Amazing
Arctic
& Antarctic
Projects
You Can Build Yourself

Carmella Van Vleet

Illustrated by Steven Weinberg

To Jane and Beth, who've never left me out in the cold.

Nomad Press
A division of Nomad Communications
10 9 8 7 6 5 4 3 2 1
Copyright © 2008 by Nomad Press

ISBN: 978-1-9346700-9-5

Illustrations by Steven Weinberg

Questions regarding the ordering of this book should be addressed to
Independent Publishers Group
814 N. Franklin St.
Chicago, IL 60610
www.ipgbook.com

Nomad Press
2456 Christian St.
White River Junction, VT 05001

green press
INITIATIVE

Nomad Press is committed to preserving ancient forests and natural resources. We elected to print *Arctic & Antarctic Projects You Can Build Yourself* on 4,315 lb. of Rolland Enviro100 Print instead of virgin fibres paper. This reduces an ecological footprint of:

Tree(s): 37
Solid waste: 1,057kg
Water: 100,004L
Suspended particles in the water: 6.7kg
Air emissions: 2,321kg
Natural gas: 151m3

It's the equivalent of:
Tree(s): 0.8 american football field(s)
Water: a shower of 4.6 day(s)
Air emissions: emissions of 0.5 car(s) per year

Nomad Press made this paper choice because our printer, Transcontinental, is a member of Green Press Initiative, a nonprofit program dedicated to supporting authors, publishers, and suppliers in their efforts to reduce their use of fiber obtained from endangered forests.

For more information, visit www.greenpressinitiative.org

ENVIRONMENTAL CHOICE · CHOIX ENVIRONNEMENTAL

BIO GAS
ENERGY

FSC
Recycled
Supporting responsible
use of forest resources
Cert no. SW-COC-000952
www.fsc.org
© 1996 Forest Stewardship Council

Contents

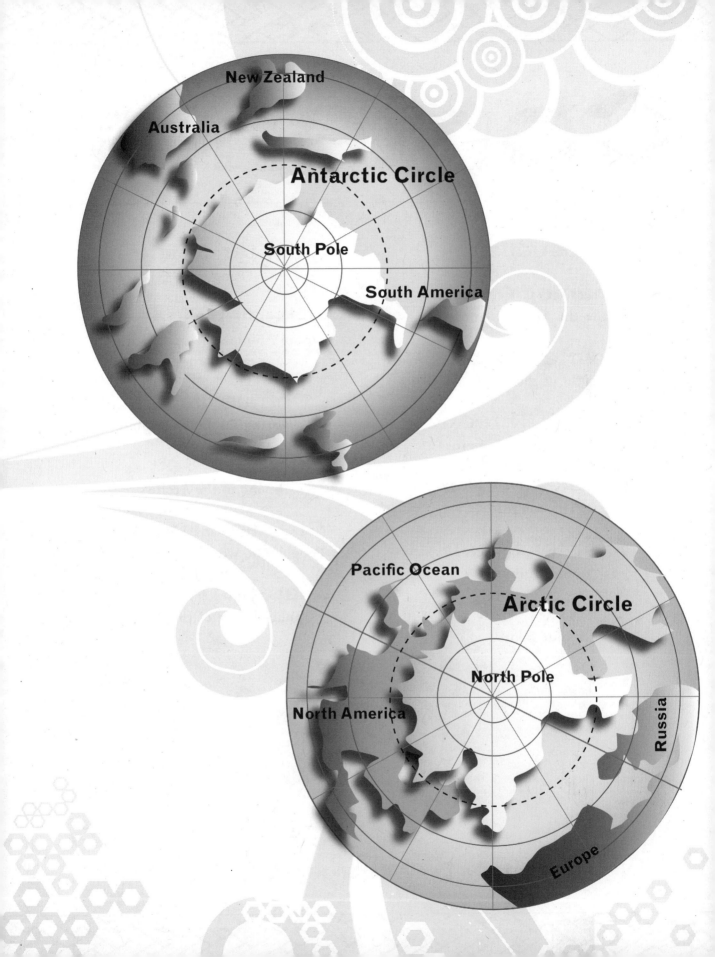

Introduction

The North and South Poles have always fascinated people. Curious explorers have braved the extreme cold to stand on both the top and go to the bottom of the world. Scientists have lugged equipment and supplies over thousands of miles of ice to study the poles and discover their frozen secrets. Many of us have watched from afar, looking at photos or reading stories, and imagined what it would be like to live where night lasts for six months. And some of us have wondered just what's so special about giant sheets of ice in the first place!

Far from being boring or "just ice," the Arctic and Antarctica are filled with all kinds of wonderful and beautiful animals, plants, people, scientific wonders, and mysteries.

In this interactive book, we'll explore things like the Arctic tundra, the Northern Lights, glaciers, frozen lakes that have been buried for 500,000 years, and animals and plants that are able to thrive in the world's harshest climates. We'll also meet the explorers who risked everything to be the first to stand on the North and South Poles, as well as the people who live or work at the top and bottom of the world today. And we'll learn some amazingly cool (pardon the pun!) science and history and discover why it's so important that we protect the polar regions.

Most of the projects in this book can be made with materials you probably have around your home or that you can find at any hardware or craft store. Many of them can also be done with very little adult help or supervision. So grab your coat, put on your snow boots, and get ready to explore the polar regions and *Build it Yourself*!

Where are the Arctic & Antarctic?

On maps or on globes, the earth is divided into two **hemispheres**, or half-spheres. The top is called the **Northern Hemisphere** and the bottom is the **Southern Hemisphere.**

In the most basic terms, the **Arctic** region is at the top of the Northern Hemisphere and the **Antarctic** is at the bottom of the Southern Hemisphere. Of course, there's a lot more to it than that!

The Arctic

The Arctic Ocean is about 5.5 million square miles of water sitting on top of the world. But the area we call the Arctic is not really a landmass. It's a giant sheet of **sea ice** that floats on top of the Arctic Ocean! Sea ice is formed by ocean water, while regular ice is formed by fresh water. The sea ice is called the **polar ice cap,** and it covers most of the Arctic Ocean.

Some of the polar ice cap is just a few feet thick, but on average, it's about ten feet thick. Some of it is perennial, meaning it stays frozen all year round. And some of it melts and then refreezes with the seasons. The amount of ice is always changing. For example, by the end of winter, there can be over 161 million square feet of ice. In late summer, there is about 86 million square feet of ice. Over the last 30 years, the polar ice cap has become smaller because of **global warming**.

The Arctic is surrounded by land in Greenland, Canada, and Russia. Parts of these countries as well as parts of Alaska are in an area we call the **Arctic Circle.** The Arctic Circle is the area inside an imaginary circle. The center of this circle is the North Pole and it extends about 1,620 miles in all directions. The single biggest landmass within the Arctic Circle is Greenland.

The Poles Can Switch Places

Another interesting thing about the magnetic poles is that they can change places with each other! We know this because we can see different magnetism in ancient rocks. Evidence shows that this happens, on average, about every 200,000 to 300,000 years. The last time it happened was nearly 800,000 years ago, though. There's no need to worry. The flipping of the magnetic poles takes thousands of years and doesn't hurt life on Earth.

did you know?
The polar ice cap is always moving. It drifts about 400 yards every hour. But if you were standing on the ice, you probably wouldn't notice it drifting because you'd be moving at the same speed.

Greenland is an island. But it's not very green! In fact, most of it, around 85 percent, is covered in a dome-shaped sheet of ice. Airplanes frequently fly over the Arctic Circle and North Pole because it is the quickest way to get from some countries to others.

The Antarctic

Unlike the Arctic, the area we call the Antarctic has a landmass, called **Antarctica**. Antarctica is one of the world's seven continents and is about 4.5 million square miles. It lies in the Southern Ocean, which is also called the Antarctic Ocean. Some of Antarctica is a large area of mountainous land. Some of it is a group of islands. We just can't see most of the land because 98 percent of it is covered by an ice sheet! This is why the scientists who work in the Antarctic have nicknamed it "The Ice."

words to know

hemisphere: half a sphere, like half a ball.

Northern Hemisphere: the top half of the globe.

Southern Hemisphere: the bottom half of the globe.

Arctic: the region at the top of the Northern Hemisphere.

Antarctic: the region at the bottom of the Southern Hemisphere.

sea ice: ice made up of ocean water.

polar ice cap: a giant sheet of sea ice that floats on top of the Arctic Ocean.

global warming: the gradual warming of the entire planet.

Arctic Circle: an imaginary circle that extends south about 1,620 miles in every direction from the geographic North Pole.

Antarctica: one of the seven continents of the world and the most southern.

The Arctic Circle and the Antarctic Circle mark the latitudes where daylight and darkness can last up to 24 hours.

Antarctic ice varies in thickness, but it is much, much thicker than Arctic ice. On average, it's 1½ miles thick, but at some places it can get up to 3 miles thick! Also, Antarctic ice is not sea ice, like Arctic ice. It is made of snow, which is fresh water. There is sea ice around the continent itself, though. This ice is called **fast ice**, and it's attached to the land and extends out from the coast like a shelf over the ocean. For this reason, fast ice is also sometimes called shelf ice. In winter, fast ice can add 1,000 miles of area from all the shores of Antarctica, which basically doubles the continent's size.

Like Arctic ice, much of this ice melts with the warmer season. For instance, during the winter, there is about 193 million square feet of ice. By the end of summer, there is only about 32 million square feet of ice in the Antarctic.

words to know

latitude: how far north or south a location is from the equator.

equator: the imaginary line running around the middle of the earth that divides it into the Northern Hemisphere and the Southern Hemisphere.

fast ice: sea ice that extends from the coasts of Antarctica like a shelf.

Antarctic Circle: an imaginary circle that extends north about 1,620 miles in every direction from the geographic South Pole.

South Pole: the southernmost point on the earth, also called the geographic South Pole.

axis: the imaginary line that the earth rotates around.

North Pole: the northernmost point on the earth, also called the geographic North Pole.

did you know?
Most of the world's fresh water—85 percent—is frozen in the Antarctic!

Just as there is an Arctic Circle, there is also an **Antarctic Circle**. The **South Pole** is at the center of the Antarctic Circle. The Antarctic Circle extends about 1,620 miles in all directions, the same distance as the Arctic Circle. But other than the continent of Antarctica, the Antarctic Circle contains no landmass. The closest continent is South America, which is about 1,600 miles away.

did you know?
The North Pole points toward the star Polaris, which is also called the North Star.

The Geographic Poles and the Magnetic Poles

Imagine the earth is a ball with a long pole going right through its middle and out its top and bottom. This imaginary pole, or line, is the earth's **axis**. The earth rotates around this axis each day. The **North Pole** is at the top of this axis. The South Pole is at the bottom of this axis. In other words, the North Pole is the northernmost point on the earth, and the South Pole is the southernmost point on Earth.

You can't place a flag or marker at the North Pole and expect it to be there in a few days, though. Remember, the Arctic ice moves. The South Pole, on the other hand, has a more permanent marker because there is land there. It's still not completely permanent though, because the ice on top of Antarctica is slowly moving, too.

words to know

magnetic field: an invisible field (or area) created by moving charges near a magnet or an electrical current.

solar wind: the stream of electrically charged particles emitted by the sun.

Magnetic North Pole: the northernmost point of the earth's magnetic field.

Magnetic South Pole: the southernmost point of the earth's magnetic field.

katabtic winds: high-speed winds that constantly race down mountain slopes.

The North and South Poles are considered the geographic poles. But they are not the only poles that are important. For example, scientists are often more concerned about where the magnetic poles are. But what are the magnetic poles?

Earth is surrounded by a **magnetic field**. This is good! The magnetic field protects us from **solar winds** and radiation from space. It exists because the earth spins at one speed, while its molten, metallic core spins at a different speed. This creates electrical currents and causes the earth to become something like a giant electromagnet. The northernmost point of the magnetic field is called the **Magnetic North Pole**. It is the point where magnetic compasses point. The southernmost point of the magnetic field is called the **Magnetic South Pole**.

Fun
Things to Try

- Calculate how far your city or state is from the Arctic or Antarctic Circle.

- Nobody knows why the storms in Antarctica are called Herbies. Write a story about how the Herbie got its name.

- The Antarctic is nicknamed "The Ice." See if you can come up with a few good nicknames for the Arctic. Take a poll and see which nickname other people like the best.

There are two interesting things about the magnetic poles. They are not near the geographic poles and they move. Their positions move an average of about 25 miles each year. They also move each day based on a variety of things such as changes in the atmosphere. Every few years, scientists calculate where the magnetic poles are. In 2005, the Magnetic North Pole was hundreds of miles south of the geographic North Pole. The Magnetic South Pole isn't calculated as often as the Magnetic North Pole, but it's exactly 180 degrees opposite from the magnetic North Pole. In the 1990s, the magnetic South Pole was just off the coast of East Antarctica, in the Antarctic Ocean.

did you know?

The North Pole and the South Pole don't belong to any country. There are several countries that are trying to claim the North Pole, however. These include Canada, Russia, the United States, Denmark, and Norway.

Brrrr... It's Cold at the Poles!

The average temperature at the North Pole is 0 degrees Fahrenheit. The average temperature at the South Pole is –60 degrees Fahrenheit. But if you were to visit the Arctic or Antarctic, the extreme cold and frostbite aren't the only things you'd have to worry about. Because the sun reflects off the ice, visitors must take precautions against sunburn and snow blindness. Snow blindness is a temporary condition caused when the cornea of the eye is sunburned. Another problem is altitude sickness because much of the Arctic and Antarctic regions are thousands of feet above sea level. And let's not forget the wind! In Antarctica, cold, dense air causes something called **katabtic winds**. These constant winds race down the mountain slopes and through valleys at over 60 mph. There are also terrible windstorms, called Herbies, with gusts up to 100 mph.

Make Your Own **Electromagnet**

Supplies

* 3-inch iron nail
* 24 to 36 inches of insulated copper wire
* scissors
* new, D size battery
* electrical tape
* a few paper clips and other small metal objects

1 Wrap the wire tightly around the nail as many times as you can without overlapping the wire. It is important to leave about a quarter inch on both ends of the nail exposed. Leave 5 inches of wire loose at each end. If you have extra wire, just cut it off.

2 Use the scissors to carefully strip the coating off the loose ends of the wire. Tape one of the loose wires to the top of the battery. Tape the other loose wire to the bottom of the battery.

3 Hold a paper clip close to one end of the nail. Your electromagnet should attract the paper clip. Experiment with other small, metal objects and see what else the electromagnet attracts.

4 When you're done experimenting, be sure to take the ends of the wire off the battery. **Be careful**, because the wire may have become hot!

Make Your Own **Compass**

1 Fill the dish with about an inch of water. Place the milk lid in the middle. It doesn't matter if it's face up or face down, just as long as it floats.

2 Rub the north end of the bar magnet along the needle. Move from the eye of the needle to the point in a loop. Do not rub the magnet back and forth. You need to move the magnet in one direction for this to work. Do this approximately 20 times.

3 Carefully lay the needle on top of the milk lid. Watch what happens! The needle's point should slowly move to point north.

Supplies

* glass or aluminum pie dish
* water
* plastic lid off a gallon milk jug
* bar magnet, marked with north and south
* sewing needle

Light at the
Poles

Some of the neatest things about the polar regions have to do with light. For example, the North and South Poles experience 24 hours of light or darkness for months at a time. Imagine not knowing if it was morning or night unless you looked at a clock! How does this happen?

Like the other planets in our solar system, the earth travels around the sun, and spins on its axis. The earth's axis isn't perfectly straight up and down, though. It tilts a bit. So the poles are tilted toward or away from the sun during certain parts of the year. Because the poles are on opposite ends of the earth, this means that when the North Pole and Arctic Circle are tilted toward the sun, the South Pole and Antarctic Circle are tilted away from the sun.

On December 21, the Northern Hemisphere has its winter **solstice.** This means that the North Pole is as far away from the sun as it can get. In the Northern Hemisphere, it is the day with the least amount of sunlight, but the Arctic Circle is so far north that the sun doesn't reach it at all. This is winter in the Northern Hemisphere and summer in the Southern Hemisphere. By June 21, the Northern Hemisphere's summer solstice, the situation is reversed. The Antarctic Circle is dark and experiencing winter while the Arctic Circle is bright and enjoying summer.

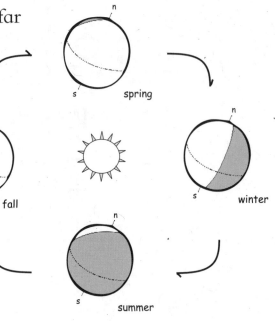

During the Arctic's summer, the sun moves down towards the horizon, but never sets. The result is what's called the midnight sun. During this time, the sky has a constant, soft glow and colorful bands of light (like those in sunrises and sunsets) streak across the horizon. The same thing happens in the Antarctic during its summer. When one polar region is experiencing the midnight sun, the other is experiencing what's known as polar night. Polar night is when the sun stays below the horizon and there is constant darkness or dusk.

did you know?
The midnight sun means the sun is literally up at midnight!

The poles don't always experience either all sunlight or all darkness. As the earth spins and travels around the sun, different amounts of sunlight hit the polar regions. For instance, one day in winter the North Pole may have no light and then the next day, there will be a small period of time when there is sun. That means spring and summer are coming! Meanwhile, in the Antarctic Circle, the amount of darkness is increasing day by day.

Is there a time when the sun is shining on both poles equally? Yes. This happens during the **equinoxes**. The equinoxes occur around March 20 and September 21. These are the days of the year when the sun is

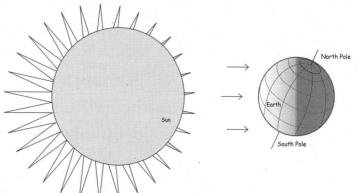

directly over the equator. The equator is the imaginary line that circles the middle of the earth and divides the Northern and Southern Hemispheres. On these days, the amount of sunlight and darkness (or day and night) are of equal length everywhere on Earth.

Light Tricks and Light Shows

White nights, polar nights, and midnight suns are not the only interesting phenomenon at the polar regions. There are several really cool things caused by cold air, bending light, ice crystals, and crashing atoms.

Imagine you are looking out over the Arctic ice and see an iceberg floating in the sky. Or maybe you're exploring Antarctica and see a building that you know isn't there. You're probably seeing a mirage. A mirage is an optical illusion, a trick your eyes play on your brain, where things appear differently than they really are. Many people think mirages happen only in hot deserts.

White Nights

Areas near the Arctic and Antarctic Circles experience white nights. This happens around the summer solstice when the sun stays at the horizon or a little below it. During this time, there is enough light to be outside and do normal activities during the night. Some places that experience white nights celebrate the time. In St. Petersburg, Russia, for example, white nights happen around the time from June 11 through July 2 and are marked with a huge arts festival.

But they are common at the poles, too. And there's a very good reason for this: temperature inversions.

Temperature inversions are when air temperatures don't follow the normal pattern. Normally, you expect the air to get colder the higher you go in altitude. But at the poles, the opposite is sometimes true. This is because the snow and ice cool the layer of air that's close to the ground but not the layer of air that's higher up. The result is that the lower and upper air layers have different temperatures and therefore, densities. These different densities bend light so that it follows the earth's curve instead of going straight. But our brains don't care if the light was bent or not; it still thinks it was sent in straight lines. This means we may see things floating in the sky, upside down, or smaller or bigger than they are. We can even see things that are very far away because the light can bend over the horizon.

Halos are another interesting phenomenon you can see at the poles. Halos often look like rings of light or color that surround the sun and moon. They are caused by light being bent as it shines through cirrus clouds, which are composed of ice crystals.

Sun dogs (sometimes called parhelia or mock suns) are patches of colored light that appear next to the sun. They are a kind of halo and often appear in pairs, one on either side of the sun. Halos can also be formed by light shining through diamond dust. Diamond

words to know

solstice: the two times of the year when the sun is at its highest and lowest points in the sky.

equinox: the two days of the year when days and nights are equal lengths.

halos: displays of light that are created when light is bent while going through ice crystals or cirrus clouds. They often look like rings or light or color around the sun or moon.

dust is the name of the water crystals in the air that are flash frozen by the extreme cold of the polar regions. Diamond dust, which is finer than snowflakes, floats in the air and sparkles like its name suggests.

The most famous light phenomenon at or near the poles are **auroras**. The aurora borealis, also known as the **Northern Lights**, and the aurora australis, known as the **Southern Lights**, are spectacular and colorful lightshows put on by nature. They have been described as ribbons of light, rippling curtains of colors, waterfalls of light and color, and crowns of light. And colorful is right! Auroras can have a wide range of colors, from an eerie green or neon pink to blue and red.

did you know?
Auroras occur on other planets too, including Jupiter, Saturn, Neptune and Mars.

They have two basic formations: curtain and corona. A curtain aurora looks like a curtain in a breeze. A corona aurora has rays that move outward. Auroras also sometimes look like a ring or crown of light. They occur 24 hours a day, but are most visible to us against the night sky.

Auroras are caused by **atoms** colliding with the earth's **atmosphere**. Solar wind is a stream of electrically charged atoms that are pushed through space when the sun's atmosphere expands. When these charged atoms hit the edge of earth's atmosphere they transfer energy. This makes the atoms light up.

The reaction goes from atom to atom and this causes the rippling effect. What colors are produced depends on what kind of atoms collide or where in the atmosphere they hit. Oxygen atoms that hit lower in the atmosphere result in a yellow-green. This is the most common color in auroras. Oxygen atoms that hit higher in the atmosphere result in a rare, red color. Nitrogen atoms cause the bluish light of auroras.

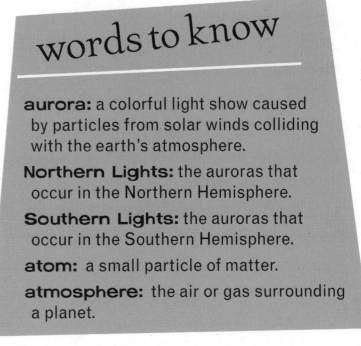

words to know

aurora: a colorful light show caused by particles from solar winds colliding with the earth's atmosphere.

Northern Lights: the auroras that occur in the Northern Hemisphere.

Southern Lights: the auroras that occur in the Southern Hemisphere.

atom: a small particle of matter.

atmosphere: the air or gas surrounding a planet.

Auroras can be seen at both poles and in countries just south of the Arctic Circle and sometimes in areas just north of the Antarctic Circle. They are lovely to see, but the same charged particles that create them can cause problems with satellites, radio communications, and even electrical systems. This is one of the reasons why scientists study auroras. Scientists also study them to learn more about the earth's atmosphere because it helps protect the planet.

Fun
Things to Try

- Which would you rather experience: polar nights or the midnight sun? Why? Take a survey and see what your friends and family would choose.

- Next time there are thin, cirrus clouds in the winter sky, keep an eye out for sun dogs. You can see them in most areas of the United States.

Make Your Own **Bending Light**

1 Fill the glass with water about two-thirds full.

2 Place the pencil inside the middle of the glass and look at it from the front of the glass. Does the pencil appear straight?

3 Move the pencil so it leans against the edge of the glass. Look at the pencil through the front of the glass again. Now, the pencil appears broken. This is because the water is bending the light. Neat, eh?

Supplies

* tall, clear glass
* water
* pencil

Supplies

* small, shallow bowl that you can't see through
* penny
* water
* a friend to help you

1 Place the penny in the middle of the bowl. Stand above the bowl and look directly down at the penny.

2 Slowly walk backwards. Keep your eye on the penny and keep walking backwards until you can't see the penny at all.

3 When you can't see the penny, stop walking. Keep your head as still as you can.

4 Have your friend hold the penny down with a finger and fill the bowl with water about two-thirds full. Now have the friend carefully move his or her finger off the penny. You should be able to see the penny even though your head and the penny didn't move!

5 Don't keep the fun all to yourself. Switch places with your friend and let him or her try the experiment!

Make Your Own
Northern Lights Picture

Supplies

* ❄ black construction paper
* ❄ construction paper in any color, the same size as the black piece
* ❄ colored chalk, several colors
* ❄ cotton balls

1 Place your piece of black construction paper down on your work area. It should be turned lengthwise.

2 Carefully tear the second piece of construction paper lengthwise. Important: you don't want a straight line! Tear your piece of paper so it looks like big and small waves or mountains without pointy peaks.

3 Next, lay the torn piece of paper lengthwise on top of the black piece. You want the torn piece to be about one or two inches from the top of the black piece of paper.

4 Take a piece of chalk and trace all along the torn edge. Pick up the torn piece of paper. Use a cotton ball to gently blend the chalk dust downward (about 1½ to 2 inches) on the black piece of paper.

5 Place the torn edge of the torn piece of paper near where the chalk starts to fade. Lay it down and gently press along the torn edge.

6 Use a different colored chalk piece to trace the torn edge. When you're done, use the cotton ball to blend the color downward.

7 Keep moving the torn piece of paper down the black piece of paper and tracing the edge of the torn paper as before. Use a different colored chalk piece each time.

8 Leave a few inches of the black paper blank near the bottom. This blank space will be your sky's horizon.

9 When you have all the layers of color you'd like, use the cotton ball to gently blend the edges of colors together. Now, your picture should look like a curtain aurora with its rippling and blending colors!

Ice, Glaciers and Icebergs

Water is unique. It is the only substance that is less dense as a solid—ice—than as a liquid. This is why ice floats. If it didn't, the Arctic and the Antarctic wouldn't exist, at least not in the way we know them to exist.

The Arctic and Antarctic are covered in sheet ice. Unlike what the name suggests, sheet ice is not a thin, flat piece of ice. The ice at the poles has ridges and cracks and interesting formations called ridges. It is constantly changing. Of course, the ice doesn't magically appear this way. The wind and waves help create these features. And there are stages of ice formation. Both the Arctic's sea ice and the Antarctic's fast ice are created in stages.

Water normally freezes at 32 degrees Fahrenheit. But saltwater freezes at a lower temperature, around 29 degrees Fahrenheit. When it's cold enough, the ocean's surface begins to freeze into ice crystals called

words to know

grease ice: a slushy, soupy ice that leaves an oily sheen on top of the water. It is the first stage of sea ice.

nilas: the second stage of sea ice formation, this thin, flexible sheet of ice moves with the waves.

pancake ice: the third stage of sea ice. These large plates of ice bump into each other and cause the edges to turn up.

floe: large, flat pieces of sea ice.

firn: grain-like snow crystals.

grease ice. This is a slushy, soupy kind of ice. It leaves an oily sheen on the top of the water, thus the name.

As the temperature drops, more ice crystals form. These crystals stick together and form a thin, flexible sheet of ice called a **nilas**. Nilas ice moves with the waves. As it gets colder and the water freezes further, the nilas becomes thicker and thicker. As the ocean waves compress it, nilas ice forms into large plates called **pancake ice.** These rounded pieces of ice move around and bump into each other causing the edges to turn up slightly.

As the temperature gets lower and lower, the pancake ice gets thicker and bigger. Eventually, the ocean compresses these plates into large, flat masses of ice. These are called **floes**.

Floes can be anywhere from 60 feet wide to 6 miles wide. Ocean currents and wind move floes across the water slowly. Even though they are moving slowly, floes crash into each other with a good deal of force. These collisions form ridges. Part of the ice is pushed up and looks kind of like a pile of blocks. Ridges can be six feet tall or even taller. Some of the ice is pushed under the water. These pieces are called keels. In the summer, as the temperatures get warmer, the edges of ridges melt. The result is a snow hill called a hummock.

When people first started exploring the poles, their ships got stuck in the ice-packed waters. With no way to get food or other supplies, many explores died. Today, specially designed ships called icebreakers make way for other ships by plowing through the ice with rounded bows and reinforced hulls.

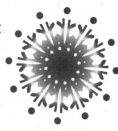

Glaciers and Icebergs

The snow that falls at the polar regions doesn't get a chance to melt because it's so cold there. So what happens when new snow keeps falling on top of old snow?

Snow crystals are feathery, six-sided crystals. But when new snow keeps falling on old snow, the bottom snow is compressed. The pointy sides of the snow crystals are broken off and the crystal is rounded into tiny grains called **firn**.

did you know?
Glaciers can be hundreds of feet high!

These grains have bubbles of air, but as the weight of the new snow continues to compress the old snow, the trapped air is squished out more and more. So instead of being fluffy, the snow becomes hard, bluish ice. The ice looks blue because it has been squeezed so tightly that there is little air inside. With little or no air, the sunlight can't be scattered. (Scattered light looks white to us.) This means sunlight can travel deeper into the ice. And as the light travels deeper into it, the ice absorbs more of the red end of the light spectrum. That leaves the light at the blue end of the spectrum left to bounce back to our eyes.

After thousands of years of snow and compression, the ice field finally gets so large and heavy that it begins to move. Once it starts to move, it becomes a **glacier**. Glaciers usually move downhill. They move in two ways. One way is called creeping. Creeping means the layers of ice crystals glide or slide over each other. The second way is called sliding. This is when the glacier slides over a thin layer of melted water called melt ice. All glaciers move in both ways, but they usually travel in one of the ways more often.

Glaciers can move as slowly as a couple of inches a year or as fast as two hundred feet a day! Most travel so slowly, though, that we can't see them move. How fast a glacier moves depends on a variety of factors: what it's sitting on top of (water, melt ice, or land), how big the glacier is, and how heavy it is. When glaciers move, they make lots of noises. The compressed ice moans and groans and pops. As you can imagine, it might be pretty

More Than Just Ice

The ice at the North and South Poles is kind of like a natural time capsule. Since it has been around for thousands of years, it can tell us all kinds of things about the past, including what the climate was like. Scientists use special drills to cut long, pole-shaped pieces of ice. These are called ice cores. Summer ice and winter ice look like alternating bands of light and dark on the cores. Summer's daylight causes the ice to melt a little and the nighttime temperatures then freeze it again. This creates a layer of ice crystals called hoarfrost, which are the light bands. Scientists can tell how old ice is by counting these bands.

Scientists also study things like minerals and particles in the ice. The National Ice Core Laboratory in Colorado stores many ice cores for scientists to study.

unnerving to stand so close to something that sounds like it's going to crack and fall down at any moment!

As glaciers move, the tops of them crack. These cracks are called crevasses. Crevasses can happen in any kind of ice, not just glaciers. Some crevasses may be only a few feet wide but they can also be hundreds of feet deep. For that reason, they are very dangerous. Unfortunately, they aren't always easy to see. Sometimes, an arch of snow called a snow bridge hides the crevasse.

did you know?
A snow bridge hiding a crevasse on an airport runway in Antarctica once partially swallowed a small plane! Fortunately, everyone on the plane was unhurt.

Most of the world's glaciers are in Antarctica. Glaciers are not unique to the poles, though. They can happen anywhere where snow doesn't have a chance to melt. There are glaciers high in mountains in Alaska and the Canada Rockies, for example. As glaciers move, they change the landscape. They can flatten and smooth everything in their path. They can also pick up rocks, which then scratch the bedrock and leave rack-like grooves.

Once glaciers hit water, they can break apart. This is called **calving**. Broken pieces of a glacier are called icebergs. Icebergs come in

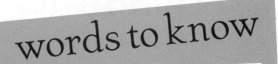

glacier: a very large field of fresh water ice that is moving.
calving: the breaking apart of a glacier.

different sizes. For instance, small ones, called growlers, can be the size of a pickup truck. Growlers get their name because the ice seems to growl. Medium-sized ones can be the size of a small office building. Big icebergs can even be the size of a small state! What's special about icebergs is that they are mostly underwater. You can see only the tops of some icebergs and have no idea just how big they really are underneath the water's surface. This makes icebergs extremely dangerous to ships.

Ever heard of the RMS *Titanic*? On its first trip in 1912, this famous ship hit a medium-sized iceberg in the Atlantic Ocean and sank, killing over 1,500 people. After the *Titanic* sank, an International Ice Patrol was formed. At first, they tried breaking up icebergs by blowing them up or melting them by covering them. When those things didn't work, they decided to study icebergs instead. By studying the paths of icebergs, they could warn ships to be on the lookout. Today, airplanes and a computer system called the Iceberg Data Management and Prediction System helps the Ice Patrol track icebergs.

Fun
Things to Try

- Scientists look at ice as a kind of natural time capsule. Why not make your own time capsule?

- Now that you know that only a small part of some icebergs are visible above the water, it's easy to see where the expression (or idiom) "the tip of the iceberg" comes from. What are some other idioms you've heard? Research where they come from.

- Read up on the *Titanic*, the famous ship that was supposed to be "unsinkable!"

Make Your Own
Sinking Ice

Supplies

* ❋ 2 tablespoons water
* ❋ 2 teaspoons table salt
* ❋ plastic baggie that seals
* ❋ Styrofoam cup
* ❋ ice cubes
* ❋ freezer
* ❋ small glass

1 Put 2 tablespoons water and the salt in the plastic bag. Seal the bag and shake it to mix the ingredients. Shake until all or most of the salt dissolves. This may take a few minutes.

2 Fill the bottom of the Styrofoam cup with a couple of ice cubes. Place the baggie with the salt water on top of the ice cubes. Make sure the outside of the baggie is dry or it will stick to the ice cubes. Put one or two more ice cubes on the top of the baggie.

3 Place the cup in the freezer. Saltwater freezes at a lower temperature than plain water so be sure to put your baggie in the coldest part of your freezer (usually in the back). You may even need to lower your freezer's temperature. **Be sure to ask permission before you do this.** Allow your ice cube to freeze until it's solid or nearly solid. This may take several days because of the salt.

4 Fill the glass about halfway full with cool water. Using a glass will allow everyone to see the ice actually sink. Carefully remove the ice from the baggie. The ice may be a little slushy in spots. Ask your friends or family to predict whether or not the ice will sink or float.

5 Drop the ice into the water and watch your friends be amazed!

Make Your Own
Ice Core Sample

Supplies

❄ 16-ounce orange juice can, empty and clean

❄ water

❄ small bits of material such as sand, rice, twigs, grass

❄ blue or gray food coloring

❄ freezer

❄ scissors

❄ cookie sheet

1 Fill the orange juice can with about an inch of water. You can add a few grains of sand, rice, or bits of twigs or grass to represent plants and animal fossils or other particles that might be found in Arctic and Antarctic ice.

2 Place the can in the freezer and allow the water to freeze solid. Add another inch of water on top of the ice. Add a few drops of food coloring. Add various materials if you'd like. The food coloring will make the layer dark, like the winter ice found in real ice core samples.

3 Place the can back into the freezer and allow the second layer to become solid. Continue creating layers with water and freezing. Be sure to leave about two inches at the top of the can because the ice will expand, and because you'll need enough can to cut.

4 When your core is solid, remove it from the freezer. Use the scissors to cut a line down the top of the can.

5 Peel the can away from the ice. If it sticks, run the can and ice under some warm water for a few seconds to loosen things.

6 Next, place your ice core sample on the baking sheet and pretend you're an Arctic or Antarctic scientist!

The Tundra

What do you think of when you hear the word "tundra"? Many people think of ice, cold weather, and a flat, boring landscape. Sure, the Arctic tundra has ice and cold. But it's far from boring!

At over 5 million square miles, the **Arctic tundra** is one of the world's largest biomes. A **biome** is a particular climate with unique plants and animals. Deserts and rainforests are other examples of biomes. The Arctic tundra encircles the North Pole and extends down to where the forest takes over in North America, Europe, and other areas in the Arctic Circle.

Tundra comes from a Russian word that means "treeless plain." Besides having no trees, the tundra is mostly flat and extremely cold. The average winter temperature is minus 30 degrees Fahrenheit. And the average summer temperature range is only 37 to 55 degrees Fahrenheit. It doesn't have a lot of different types of animals, although it does have some.

It has simple vegetation and limited water drainage. It also has a short growth season, from June to August. In addition, the Arctic tundra receives only about 5 to 10 inches of **precipitation** a year.

Another really interesting thing about the Arctic tundra is its **permafrost** layer. The permafrost is just below the land surface and is usually about 10 inches to 3 feet thick. It's made up of mostly gravel, sand, and other fine, earth material.

Permafrost has a very important job. It helps provide water for the tundra. You might be surprised to hear just how it does this. Because the ground is always frozen, the summer's melting snow can't seep down very far. All of the water stays in the top layer of soil. It's this top layer of soil, called the active layer, where everything comes to life in the summer.

The tundra's active layer is anywhere from 12 to 40 inches thick. That's way too shallow for trees to take root, but enough room for a variety of plants to grow. In fact, the tundra has about 1,700 different kinds of plants!

did you know?
Permafrost is just what it sounds like—a layer of soil that's permanently frozen!

For example, the tundra is home to plants such as primrose, blue-spiked-lupine, wild crocus, slipperwort, and Arctic poppy. These flowers help paint the summer tundra landscape in beautiful yellows, blues, reds, pinks, and purples.

Because Arctic plants grow in such a harsh environment, they must adapt. One adaptation is to grow low to the ground and in tussocks.

words to know

Arctic tundra: the treeless area that encircles the North Pole and extends down to the forest areas of North America, Europe, and other areas in the Arctic Circle.

biome: a particular climate and its plants and animals. Deserts and rainforests are examples of biomes.

precipitation: rain or snow.

permafrost: a layer of soil in the Arctic Circle that's permanently frozen.

Tussocks are clumps, or bunches, of plants. Growing low to the ground helps keep plants out of the cold wind. And clumping together helps plants keep warm.

Another way plants adapt in the Arctic is to have fuzzy, dark stems. Dark stems absorb heat. And the fuzz (or tiny hairs) help trap and hold onto heat. Small, fleshy leaves can also help trap heat and moisture.

Plants must figure out a way to reproduce in a different way, too. This is because there are so few insects for pollination. Some Arctic plants rely on the wind scattering their seeds. Others send out long stems called runners and small buds called bulbils.

Another really interesting thing about the tundra is its surface designs.

did you know?
Disc-like flowers, which look like tiny satellite dishes, collect light and heat as they follow the sun across the sky each day.

These designs are caused by—what else?—ice! The changing seasons cause the active layer of the tundra to thaw and freeze, contract and expand. All this expanding and contracting causes cracks in the soil. These cracks fill with

Protecting the Permafrost

The Arctic's permafrost affects plants and animals. It also affects manmade things. For example, all the freezing and thawing sometimes cause things like buildings and telephone poles to lean. Another thing it affects is the Alaskan Pipeline.

The Alaskan Pipeline moves heated oil across 800 miles of land, most of which has permafrost. The oil must be heated so it doesn't freeze in the frigid temperatures. In order to help protect the permafrost, the pipeline runs above the ground's surface wherever possible. More than 400 miles of the pipeline is above ground. When the pipeline must be buried underground, the oil runs along special coolant pipes. These pipes help reduce the amount of heat that escapes from the oil pipe. This helps keep the permafrost from melting.

water. The water freezes into ice wedges. In the spring, the tops of the ice wedges melt and make a bigger crack. The following winter, the larger crack fills back up with ice. This whole process keeps repeating until finally the ice wedges push the soil around them up into ridges. These ridges form block-like patterns called tundra polygons.

Sometimes ice wedges make lakes. This happens when the top of the ice wedge melts and forms a shallow pool or when intersecting polygons fill with water. The sun heats the water in these pools. This, in turn, causes the frozen ground to melt more and eventually the pool gets bigger. These pools are called thermokarst lakes.

What about Antarctica?

Most of Antarctica is covered in ice—98 percent in fact. But what would you find in the 2 percent that isn't covered in ice? Well, for one, you'd find the Dry Valleys. The **Dry Valleys** are extremely cold areas of dry bare rock and soil located just west of McMurdo Sound on East Antarctica. They are bare because the mountains block the ice cap. Along with the extreme cold, mountain winds prevent any trees, shrubs or flowering plants from growing.

But the winds do help create something that is very interesting and really cool to look at—ventifacts. **Ventifacts** are rocks that have been smoothed and shaped over time by wind and ice crystals. In other parts of the world, water also helps shapes ventifacts. Sometimes, these rocks have a simple shape. For example, they may look like a pyramid. Sometimes, they are much more elaborate, like some kind of wild art sculpture!

It might sound strange, but the Dry Valleys have lakes. They are not your typical lakes, though. These lakes are covered in ice year-round. Organisms live in the lakes, and have figured out how to exist in the cold and dark water.

Even though it hasn't rained here in thousands of years, the Dry Valleys have plant life. There are about

words to know

Dry Valleys: extremely cold mountain valleys with dry, bare rock and soil. The Dry Valleys are located just west of McMurdo Sound on East Antarctica.

ventifacts: rocks that have been smoothed and shaped over time by wind and ice crystals.

did you know?
Lake Vostok, under a Russian research station near the Magnetic South Pole, has been frozen and buried miles under ice for at least 500,000 years.

Volcanos

Antarctica is also home to many volcanoes. Mount Erebus is the continent's most active volcano, erupting several times a day. It's located on Ross Island and is nearly 12,450 feet high. It is a stratovolcano, meaning it's a tall, cone-shaped volcano. In 1908, an explorer named Ernest Shackleton and his crew climbed its summit.

The volcano fascinates scientists as well as explorers. It's the world's southernmost active volcano. It is also one of the few in the world that has an exposed lava lake inside its crater. (Mount Erebus' crater is 2,130 feet across.) Since most volcanoes have covered chambers, the open lava gives scientists a chance to study the molten rock more closely. But not too closely. After all, the lava is 1,700 degrees Fahrenheit.

80 varieties of plant life in Antarctica, including lichens, mosses, and liverworsts. Of these three, lichens are the most common. Lichens are plants that combine two types of organisms—fungi and algae. Lichens are black, gray, or brown. They look like a bunch of dried-out grass and don't have flowers. One of the reasons lichens can survive in such a harsh environment is because they can shut down their metabolism when they need to. This means they can stop using nutrients and simply store them. Lichens grow mainly on rocks. Antarctic mosses, on the other hand, often grow *inside* rocks, where there is more humidity.

Like plants in the Arctic, Antarctic plants grow together in clumps for protection from the cold and wind. The only vascular plants, meaning plants with stems, roots, and leaves, are Antarctic pearlwort and hair grass.

Make Your Own
Ice Wedge Popsicle

1 Fill the cup about two-thirds full with rice. Put your finger in a corner of the plastic bag. Gently push the corner of the bag down into the rice. This will make your wedge.

2 Once you've made a small wedge in the rice, take your finger out of the bag. Put the spoon inside the bag and use it to gently push the rice aside to make the wedge bigger. Be careful not to poke a hole in the bag with the spoon. When you're done, fold the rest of the bag over the cup's rim to protect the rice.

3 Fill the wedge with juice. The liquid should be level with the top of the rice. Place a small piece of foil over the top of the cup. Carefully poke the craft stick through the middle of the foil and into the juice.

Supplies

* ❋ paper or plastic cup (don't use glass)
* ❋ 1 to 2 cups of uncooked rice
* ❋ plastic bag, sandwich size
* ❋ spoon
* ❋ fruit juice
* ❋ foil
* ❋ wooden craft stick
* ❋ freezer

More — Things to Try

* Learn more about some of the world's other biomes, such as a rainforest or desert.
* Create your own ventifact with clay.

4 Now, place the cup in the freezer and wait a few hours. When the juice is frozen, pull the plastic bag out of the rice. (If the rice didn't get wet, you can reuse it.) To remove your ice wedge Popsicle from the plastic, run it under warm water for 15 to 30 seconds. Then, enjoy your Arctic treat!

Make Your Own
Model of Mount Erebus

1 Cut the plastic tub in half so it makes a shallow dish that's about 1½ inches high. This will be your volcano's crater.

2 Cut the top one-third of your milk jug off. Keep the lid on but don't cut off the handle. You won't need the bottom of the milk jug so you can recycle it.

3 Set the plastic dish on top of the milk jug's lid. Use a few pieces of masking tape to attach it there. This will be your volcano's base. Set your volcano base on a large piece of waxed paper.

4 Use scrunched up pieces of foil to fill in the spaces around the jug's handle and under the plastic tub. You are making a volcano-shaped base for your clay.

Volcano Supplies

❋ small plastic tub such as a margarine container, cleaned and dried

❋ scissors

❋ gallon milk jug with its lid, cleaned and dried

❋ masking tape

❋ waxed paper

❋ foil

❋ 4 cups flour

❋ 1½ cups salt

❋ 1 teaspoon alum, found with the spices in the grocery store

❋ 1½ to 2 cups water

❋ spoon and bowl

❋ white and black craft paint

❋ white glitter, optional

5 To make the clay, mix the flour, salt, alum, and 1½ cups of water in the bowl. Mix the dough as well as you can with the spoon. After the dough has started to stick together, add a few teaspoons of water and knead the dough with your hands. Keep adding water a little bit at a time and kneading until the dough becomes stiff but workable.

6 Cover the volcano base completely with clay. You can spread a little bit of dough around the edge of the plastic tub, but don't put any inside of it. Let the volcano dry for several days until it is hard.

7 Finally, paint your volcano white and use the black to create areas of gray or shadows. Sprinkle on some white glitter for the sparkling snow.

8 Now it's time to make the lava! Squeeze or scoop the hair gel into your plastic dish. You can add as much or as little as you'd like. Add a few drops of red food coloring to the gel and mix it in using the craft stick. Use the craft stick to pull the gel up and create peaks of lava.

Lava Supplies

❊ clear hair-styling gel

❊ red food coloring

❊ craft stick

Tundra
Animals

The tundra is also filled with some pretty fascinating animals and birds. And each of these animals is well suited to the cold environment. They use a variety of **adaptations** to survive, including large size, **camouflage**, thick fur, specialized hooves, small ears and noses, and migration. It would be difficult to cover every animal because there are so many. Over 200 species of birds alone visit the Arctic Circle each year! But here are a few of the most common and their adaptations.

"Out of my way!"

Being big and having lots of fur is one way to keep warm in the tundra. No one knows this better than the musk ox. A male musk ox can be 5 feet tall and weigh up to 700 pounds. He has strong, short legs with sharp hooves, broad shoulders, and lots of long, shaggy fur that often comes close to touching the ground. The Inuit, or native people of the Arctic, call the musk ox oomingmak, which means "animal with skin like a beard." The wool undercoat, called a quiviut, is super warm. In fact, it's the warmest natural fiber in the world. Inuit people use it to make yarn.

Musk oxen protect themselves by using their curled horns and thick skulls to ram enemies. Another way they protect themselves is by traveling in herds. When they are attacked, they stand in a group with the females and calves in the center and the males facing outward. This is usually pretty effective against Arctic wolves. Unfortunately, it also makes herds easy targets for human hunters. By the early 1900s, the musk ox population was near extinction in Alaska. In the 1930s, Congress bought a herd from Greenland and introduced the musk ox back into the **ecosystem**.

words to know

adaptations: changes an animal or plant makes (or has) in response to its environment.

camouflage: protective coloration that helps a plant or animal hide and survive in its environment.

ecosystem: a community of plants and animals living in the same area and relying on each other to survive.

Another animal that uses its size to its advantage is the moose. More than seven feet tall and weighing 1,600 pounds, moose have big, flat antlers that can be nearly 6 feet wide. Long, pointy hooves grip the ice, and hollow hairs, which trap air and act like insulation, help keep the moose warm. Unlike musk oxen, moose usually travel alone. Their diet consists of their favorite foods—Arctic and Alaskan willow, twigs, grass, and aquatic vegetation. They typically eat up to 40 pounds of vegetation a day and must get down on their knees to eat low-lying plants.

did you know?
Moose are excellent swimmers.

"Now you see me, now you don't!"

Camouflage is an effective adaptation, and it's one the Arctic hare uses well. Arctic hares are one of the largest species of hares in the world. They can grow to 28 inches in length and weigh 9 to 12 pounds. With shorter ears than other hares, they can pull their ears back to conserve body heat. Their paws, which are big and flat like snowshoes, help them move over the snow easily.

did you know?
An Arctic hare can run up to 40 miles per hour when in danger!

The distinctive feature of the Arctic hare is, well, its hair. Their fur is all white during the winter except for the tips of their ears. Being white allows them to hide in the snow. In the summer, an Arctic hare's fur turns grayish white so it can take cover in the new growth of the tundra.

Another animal that turns white in the winter is the Arctic fox. Its fur, especially its long tail, becomes bushy during the winter. In fact, the Arctic fox will often wrap its long tail around its body like a toasty scarf! During the summer months, Arctic foxes are brownish-gray. This makes it easy for the fox to creep along the tundra rocks and hunt.

Arctic foxes have short legs, short ears, and a short nose. All of these features help keep foxes from losing body heat. Around 15 inches tall, 40 inches long, and weighing 6 to 10 pounds, Arctic foxes look kind of like an oversized house cat. Despite their cute appearance, they are smart hunters who will eat just about anything. They also store away extra food for hard times in their underground dens. (Many

What's On The Menu?

Many Arctic tundra animals, especially snowy owls and Arctic foxes, depend on the lemming population for survival. Lemmings are small rodents that look like fat hamsters. They are about 3 to 6 inches long and have thick fur that changes from brown to white with the seasons. They live in underground homes called burrows. These burrows even have different "rooms" for resting, eating, and going to the bathroom. Lemmings eat plants, berries, and seeds, but just about everything else eats them.

times, these dens are used by generations of the same fox family.) In the summer, Arctic foxes dine on berries, small mammals like lemmings and voles, and birds and their eggs. In the winter, they will frequently follow polar bears out onto the ice to eat the seal meat the bears leave behind.

Happy Trails!

What do you do if the food won't come to you? If you're part of an Arctic caribou herd, you go to the food. Caribous are part of the deer family and a close relative of reindeer. Like other deer, they have antlers, which they use to fight enemies and to show off during mating season. Caribous are around 4 feet tall and weigh 300 to 375 pounds. They eat grass, lichen, and mosses. Most herds don't have to travel too far to find food, but other herds do migrate long distances to eat. For example, one herd of Caribou migrates about 3,000 miles over the tundra each year to get to their favorite grazing areas.

Another animal that is known to travel long distances for food is the snowy owl. Dressed in white feathers (or mostly white, speckled feathers if you're a female), snowy owls blend right in with their wintry environment. They are one of the largest of all owl species. They are two feet tall, weigh about six pounds, and have a wingspan of nearly five feet! They have amazing eyesight and hearing, and use sharp talons to snag prey. They mostly eat lemmings, but can also eat rabbits, fish, and other birds. Unlike most owls, who are nocturnal (active at night), snowy owls are diurnal. This means they are active both day and night. With days and nights that can last 24 hours, they have to be!

More
Things to Try

- Soldiers and hunters often use camouflage to hide in their environment. Try camouflaging yourself. Can you think of a time when blending into your surroundings might be a bad thing?

- Visit a zoo and see if they have a snowy owl or caribou exhibit.

- Design an elaborate lemming burrow. Get creative and have some fun! For example, maybe your burrow has a home theater.

Make Your Own
Arctic Fox Scarf

Arctic foxes wrap their long, fluffy tails around their bodies to keep warm. Here's a simple way to make your own scarf. If you use a sewing machine, you'll need an adult's help. Fleece can be found at any fabric store.

1 Lay the pieces of fleece in a stack on top of each other. They should all be going the same direction.

2 Pin the pieces together straight down the middle. Use the needle and thread or a sewing machine to sew a straight line next to the pins.

3 Remove the pins. Then, place a piece of masking tape over the stitches. You only need to put tape on one side. It's only a temporary guide.

4 Carefully cut both edges of the fleece to create fringe. Don't cut the masking tape. The fringe should be between a half and one inch wide.

5 When you're done cutting the fringe, remove the masking tape. Fluff up the fringe and the scarf is ready to wear!

Supplies

❋ 4 strips of white fleece, each 4 inches wide and 48 inches long

❋ scissors

❋ pins

❋ white thread

❋ sewing needle or a sewing machine

❋ masking tape

Make Your Own
Flying Snowy Owl

Supplies

❉ white poster board

❉ scissors

❉ 2 brass brads

❉ white paper lunch bag

❉ markers

❉ newspaper

❉ masking tape

❉ empty toilet paper roll

❉ white paint

❉ black pipe cleaner

❉ glue

❉ small craft or pillow feathers (optional)

❉ piece of string, about 18 inches long

1 To make wings that are about six inches long, fold the poster board and make a cut-out heart. Open the heart up and then cut in half. Each half will be a wing.

2 Carefully poke a hole in the top, middle part of the rounded end of each of the wings. Push the brads through the holes on the wings.

3 Open the paper bag. Now, poke the brads through the bag about half way down. Reach inside the bag to open the brads and attach the wings. Make sure they aren't too tight. You want your wings to move. Draw eyes and a beak for your owl just above the tops of the wings.

4 Next, wad up several pieces of newspaper and stuff them into the bag. When the bag is nearly full, fold over the top and secure it down with masking tape. You can use your hands to shape the top to curve like an owl's head.

5 Cut your empty toilet paper roll in half. Use one half to cut out two triangles. Tape these to the top of your owl for ears.

6 Cut the other half of the empty paper roll length-wise into two pieces. Carefully fold the long edges of the rolls to create flaps. The flaps can fold in or out; it's doesn't matter. These will be your owl's legs. Paint them white.

7 Cut the pipe cleaner into six pieces that are equal length. When the paint is dry, carefully poke three pieces of pipe cleaner into the bottom of the paper roll "legs." Curl them over to create your owl's talons. Then put glue along the flaps and attach them to the bottom front of the lunch bag to create legs. The long side of the roll should run parallel with the long side of the bag.

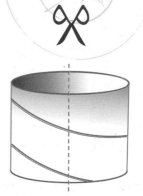

8 Now, glue feathers to the owl's wings. You can also glue feathers to the rest of the body if you'd like.

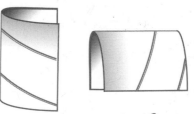

9 Finally, poke holes near the tip of each wing. Thread the ends of the string through the holes. Make a knot behind each hole so the string doesn't slip out. Now your snowy owl is ready! To get it to fly, simply pull the string up and down to flap the wings.

Polar Bears

The Arctic is filled with many animals, but none is more powerful, majestic, or feared than the polar bear. For all practical purposes, male and female polar bears are the King and Queen of the Arctic. In fact, the name Arctic comes from the Greek word *Arktikos*, meaning "country of the Great Bear."

The polar bear is called many things. His scientific name is ursus martitimus. The Inuit people call him Nanook (or Nanuk), which means "He who is without shadow." The ancient Greeks called him sea bear. Still, others call him the great white bear or simply, ice bear. But whatever you call them, one thing is for certain. Polar bears are big.

The average male polar bear (called a boar) is about eight feet from head to tail and weighs anywhere from 1,000 to 1,700 pounds. Some polar bears are even bigger, growing up to 10 feet and weighing 2,000 pounds.

That's as big as a compact car! Female polar bears (called sows) are smaller. They are six to eight feet long and weigh around 500 to 600 pounds. In the wild, polar bears live 20 to 30 years. In captivity, they live a bit longer, around 25 to 40 years. They appear all white or yellowish-white except for their black nose, black tongue, and black paw pads.

Walking Hibernation

Unlike other bears, polar bears do not hibernate. Instead, they spend the whole year roaming around the Arctic ice. They do, however, go into what scientists call **walking hibernation.** This is a state where a polar bear's metabolism and heart and breathing rate slow down as a way to conserve energy during times when food is harder to find.

Polar bears sleep about seven to eight hours every day. They spend the rest of their hours roaming the ice, searching for food, or having fun. They usually travel alone. Polar bears tend to stay on the ice, but during the warmer months they will come close to the edge of the Arctic Circle or even go below it.

Well Adapted to the Arctic

Polar bears usually walk on all fours, but can stand up and walk on their short, powerful back legs for a brief period of time. They can also run up to 35 miles per hour. To cross thin ice, they lie down flat to distribute their weight evenly over the surface and do a belly crawl. Their shuffling walking style also helps distribute their weight over ice and snow. Their paws, which can be 12 inches across, have pads that are covered in small pits that help them grip the ice. Their paws also have five sharp claws that help

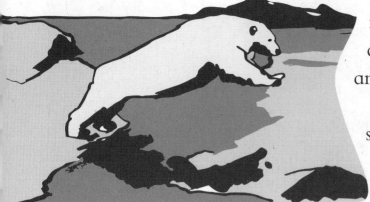

did you know?
Sometimes polar bears in zoos look green. This is because algae have started growing inside the hollow hairs of their fur.

in the slippery snow. These claws are about two inches long and are thick and curved.

In addition to no-slip paws and sharp claws, polar bears have other adaptations for living in the cold Arctic weather. For example, their small ears and tails help prevent the loss of body heat. The skin under their fur is black, which helps absorb the sun's heat. They also have a layer of fat between their skin and muscle. This layer, called **blubber,** is about three to four inches thick and acts as insulation. But by far the best thing polar bears have for keeping warm is their fur.

Polar bears have a one-to-two-inch-thick woolly undercoat of fur. The topcoat is made up of guard hairs. Guard hairs are hollow hairs made up of keratin, the same stuff that our fingernails are made of. These hollow hairs trap warm air. They also help a bear float in the water.

Friendly Bears
Polar bears are not territorial. When one bear meets another they greet each other by sniffing noses. Male polar bears will sometimes play fighting games. These fights do not become dangerous or real until mating season. A mother polar bear will also fight if she thinks another bear or animal is threatening her cubs. When a polar bear is angry, it growls or roars.

These hairs are oily and, when wet, stick together to form a waterproof barrier. It's kind of like the polar bear has a built-in wetsuit whenever he needs one. Guard hair looks white, but guess what, it isn't. It really is transparent or see-through. Polar bears look white or yellowish-white because their guard hairs are reflecting the snow.

Polar bears are **marine mammals.** They love to swim and sometimes will do it just for fun. They can hold their breath for up to a minute and have been known to swim for hundreds of miles without rest! Polar bears are also great climbers. When they are close to shores (during the warmer months), they will climb trees. They have good eyesight and their eyes can adjust to a variety of light. They also have a fantastic sense of smell. They can smell a seal from 20 miles away!

words to know

walking hibernation: a state where a polar bear's metabolism, heart, and breathing rate slow down as a way to conserve energy during times where food is harder to find.

blubber: a layer of fat under a marine mammal's skin used to help keep the animal warm.

marine mammal: an animal that gives birth, nurses its young, and can maintain a constant body temperature. It also lives in or near the sea and relies on the sea for food.

Polar Bear Life

Polar bears have no enemies other than humans armed with weapons. They can—and do—eat pretty much whatever they want. Their diet includes seals, fish, small walruses, Arctic foxes, sea birds, musk oxen, geese, caribou, and plants like grass and seaweed. But their all-time favorite food is seal. A polar bear will wait patiently, often for hours, by a seal's air hole. Sometimes they hide behind a pile of snow or lie down in a shallow hole they've dug out of the ice. Once the seal pops its head out to breathe or look around, all it takes is one swift *WHACK!* of the polar bear's paw and a quick bite behind the head for the seal

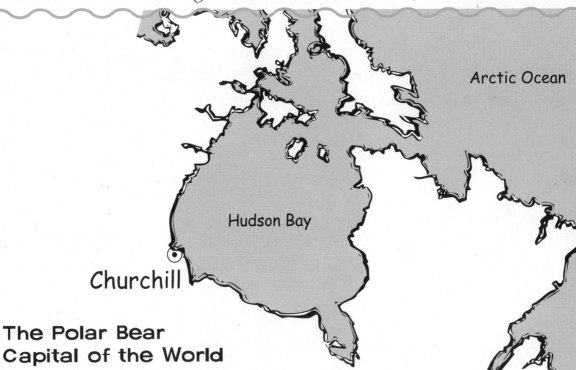

Arctic Ocean

Hudson Bay

Churchill

The Polar Bear Capital of the World

On the western shore of Hudson Bay, in Manitoba, Canada, there is a remote community called Churchill. Churchill considers itself the Polar Bear Capital of the World. Every fall, hundreds of polar bears gather near there to wait for the bay to freeze. For the most part, the bears are just hanging out, conserving energy until they can hunt again. Of course, being hungry can make anyone—or any bear—a bit cranky. Sometimes, this causes problems for the people who live in Churchill and for the thousands of tourists who visit each year to see the polar bears up close in specially designed buses.

In order to protect both man and bear, trained officials patrol the areas 24 hours a day. There are even Polar Bear Alert signs around the edges of town! When a bear gets too close, the patrol staff will try to scare it off with warning shots. If the bear continues to bother humans, it might be tranquilized and flown away by helicopter. Or it might be taken to the Polar Bear Compound, a place most folks simply call Polar Bear Jail! This is a large, windowless, steel building where polar bears can wait safely for the ice to return. Though bears in Polar Bear Jail are given water, they are not given food. This is so they don't get used to being fed by people. The people who live in Churchill love and respect polar bears. They don't want anything to happen to their big, white visitors.

to become lunch. If a polar bear is really hungry, he or she might eat the whole seal. Most times, though, a polar bear will just peal the seal's skin off, eat it, and then eat the seal's blubber before tossing the rest of the body away. (Arctic foxes and other animals eat what remains.) After a polar bear is done eating, he will lick his fur or clean up in the water. After bathing, a polar bear will shake like a dog and roll in the snow to dry off.

words to know

cub: baby bear.

threatened species: an animal whose existence is threatened.

endangered: species of animals or plants that are in danger of going extinct.

global warming: an increase in the average temperature of the earth's atmosphere, causing climatic change.

poaching: breaking the rules and hunting where and when you're not supposed to.

A female polar bear has babies once every three years. Polar bears mate during April or May. In the fall, a pregnant polar bear digs a den. These dens have an entry that's about six feet long. The den themselves are approximately five feet wide and three feet tall. They also have a fresh air vent. Around December, the mother bear gives birth to two or three **cubs**. Polar bear cubs are as small as squirrels and nearly hairless when they are born. They stay with their mother in the den, nursing and growing, for a few months. After they come out of the den, they spend the next two years with their mother, learning to hunt for themselves.

There are only about 20,000 to 40,000 polar bears in the wild and another 1,000 or so in captivity.

Make Your Own
Polar Bear Coin Collector

Supplies

❄ lots of newspaper

❄ 4 empty toilet paper rolls

❄ ruler

❄ scissors

❄ gallon milk jug with lid, clean and dried

❄ masking or white duct tape

❄ 8-ounce Styrofoam cup

❄ papier-mâché (2 cups flour mixed with 1 cup water)

❄ bowl

❄ white and black paint

❄ utility knife

1 Cover your work area with newspaper. Cut all of the toilet paper rolls so that they are three inches tall. Turn the milk jug on its side and tape the paper rolls to it. These will be your polar bear's feet.

2 Crumple up some sheets of newspaper and stuff them around the handle of the jug. Tape the paper wads in place. This is will help even out what will become your polar bear's head.

3 Turn the bear right side up so it's standing on its four feet on top of the newspaper. Place several pieces of tape about 2 inches long along the inside rim of the Styrofoam cup. Next, tape the cup over the jug's lid to make your polar bear's snout. The tape should be a hinge so the snout can be raised and lowered. Important: the tape needs to be at the *top* of where the cup and jug meet. You need to be able to move the cup so you can take out the money.

4 Tear several sections of newspaper into strips that are an inch wide and several inches long. Dip a few strips into the papier-mâché and begin laying them all around the milk jug, paper rolls, wadded newspaper and cup. **Note:** it is very important that you *don't cover* the areas where the cup and jug meet. Remember, you want your bear's snout to open and close.

5 Cover the bear in several layers of papier-mâché. Be sure to cover the legs with additional layers since the jug will be heavy when it's full of coins.

6 Allow your polar bear to completely dry. If the snout is accidentally glued to the jug, ask an adult to use a utility knife to make a seam.

7 Paint the polar bear white and give it some black eyes and a black nose. Ask an adult to help you carefully cut a slit in the top of the bear. Now, your coin collector is ready to go!

8 Once the bear is full of coins, just lift the snout out of the way, unscrew the milk jug lid and dump out the money.

did you know?
With its layer of fat and warm fur, polar bears actually have a hard time keeping cool sometimes! To cool down they might pant like a dog or jump into the icy water for a swim.

Polar bears are considered a **threatened species**. This is one step from **endangered**. The biggest threat to the polar bear is the change in climate. **Global warming** and pollution are melting the ice the bears depend on.

Another threat is hunting. For hundreds of years, people seeking a trophy or adventure have hunted polar bears. These days, international agreements have limited unnecessary hunting, but **poaching** is still a problem. Inuit people are allowed to hunt polar bears. It is part of their culture and they use all the parts they can. For example, they use the bear's fur or hides for clothing, their bones for tools, and their teeth for jewelry. Most don't eat polar bear meat, though. It has a parasite that makes you ill.

Many people are trying to help the polar bears stay off the endangered list. Scientists study polar bears by observing them or by tracking their movements with radio collars or ear tags. In order to put these devices on, a polar bear must be tranquilized. It may seem cruel, but collars and tags don't hurt the bears. Besides, this is the only safe way for humans to keep track of bears and learn about them in order to help them. Remember how big and powerful polar bears are. They might think humans are just a giant snack!

More Things to Try

- Have a friend wrap one of your hands in a plastic bag and the other one in bubble wrap. Tape around your wrists should keep everything secure. Place both hands into a bowl of ice water. The plastic should keep both your hands dry, which will help them feel comfortable. But which hand feels colder? The one with or without the air bubbles? Let your friend try next!

Penguins

If polar bears are the royalty of the Arctic, then penguins are the royalty of the Antarctic! Like polar bears, penguins have won the affection of many people. They are cute in their black and white "suits" and look playful. These short-legged, flightless birds have inspired many cartoons, books, and movies. There are 17 species of penguins, and they live in many places throughout the Southern Hemisphere. But only two species live on Antarctica. These are the **Adelie** and the **Emperor** penguins.

Adelie Penguins

The Adelie is the species most people think of when they think of penguins. Like all penguins they have a dark back and a white front. Adelies have a white ring around their eyes and are about two feet tall and weigh about 12 pounds. Because of their stiff tails, they fall into the penguin subgroup called Brush-Tailed. Other subgroups include the Crested, Banded, Giant, Little blue, and Yellow-eyed penguin.

Adelie penguins live in colonies on the edges of Antarctica and nearby islands. A **colony** is a community of penguins. There are over 150 known colonies on the continent. Some have thousands of birds! Adelie penguins spend much of the year in the ocean or traveling on the fast ice that surrounds Antarctica. The other few months of the year they spend traveling inland to nest along the rocky coasts. These nesting areas are called **rookeries**.

did you know?
The Adelie penguin was named after Terre Adelie, a place in Antarctica that French explorer Jules Dumont d'Urville named to honor his wife.

Around October (which is springtime in the Antarctic), male Adelies arrive at the nesting area a few days before the females, and carefully build a nest using small stones. Though Adelies typically return to the same nesting site year after year, there are sometimes quarrels over territory. During a disagreement, males will slap flippers or poke their beaks at one another. Penguins usually tolerate their colony neighbors though. After all, there is safety in numbers and penguins must watch out for an attack from a skua, an Antarctic bird that likes to steal penguin eggs.

When the females arrive, they search for their mate. They locate their mate in the crowded rookery by listening for his bray, or call. As you can imagine, the scene is extremely noisy!

Once the female finds the nest, she lays one or two eggs. The male takes first watch and keeps the eggs warm by covering them with his body while the female goes off to eat for a week or so. Then she returns to take her turn with the eggs so the male can eat. Moms and dads continue to take turns caring for the chicks until the eggs hatch in December. Like all birds, they feed their babies by regurgitating food into their mouths. Penguins eat mainly small fish and krell, a shrimp-like creature.

words to know

Adelie: one of the two species of penguins that live on Antarctica.

Emperor: one of the two species of penguins that live on Antarctica.

colony: a community of penguins.

rookeries: areas where penguins set up nests.

down: soft, fine feathers.

did you know?
Up to 90 percent of Adelie penguins choose the same mate each year.

When they are born, the chicks are covered in a soft fur called **down**. They grow feathers and get bigger very quickly. Within just a few weeks of hatching, they are almost adult-size. And by the time they are nine weeks old, they are ready to head out to sea and hunt for themselves.

Around January, as the Antarctic summer starts to fade, the colony will begin its migration north to their favorite feeding areas. Adelies travel north because they don't see well in the dark, and there are more daylight hours in the north.

On this journey, Adelies travel by swimming and sliding over ice floes on their bellies. This sliding looks like someone sledding on a **toboggan** so it's called tobogganing. Since Adelies can only waddle about one mile an hour, tobogganing is much faster than walking and uses less energy.

Saving energy is important since the penguins sometimes travel 1,000 miles away from their nesting grounds. Of course, humans have never been able to actually follow the penguins along their journey. The ice floes would be too dangerous for us. Instead, scientists attach special sensors to the penguin's legs to see how far they travel.

There are an estimated 2.5 million pairs of Adelie penguins in the world, but those numbers are dwindling. Adelies are what scientists call an **indicator species.** An indicator species is a species of animal so sensitive that even a tiny change in the environment can put the species in danger.

did you know?
The Blue penguin, which lives farther north and stands about 12 inches tall and weighs just three pounds, is the smallest species of penguin.

Emperors: The Big Daddy of Them All

Emperor penguins are another species of penguins that many people are familiar with. This is because of their size. Emperors are the biggest penguins. They average between 60 and 90 pounds and are about 3.8 feet tall, about the same height as an average seven-year-old human!

Their large size helps protect them from the cold. Emperors have a dark, bluish-gray back and a yellow patch around their ears that fades into their white breast feathers. They spend almost all of their time in the ocean. Most of their 40 known colonies are formed on sea ice.

Emperor penguins aren't like other penguins when it comes to breeding. Instead of laying eggs when it's warm, Emperor penguins lay eggs and raise their young in the middle of the brutally harsh, Antarctic winter. Having their chicks at this time gives the chicks plenty of time to grow before they have to venture out on their own. Of course, the wintry season makes having and raising chicks a real challenge. This is why Emperor penguins only breed two out of every three years. In May or June, which is wintertime in Antarctica, Emperors lay one egg. It is pear-shaped and about six inches long. Emperors don't build a nest. The males balance the egg on top of their feet and cover it with a patch of skin called a brood pouch. While the male incubates the egg for the next nine weeks, the female

words to know

toboggan: a kind of sled.

indicator species: an animal so in tune with its environment that even a tiny change in the environment can put the species in danger.

molting: process in which a bird's old feathers are pushed out by new feathers growing in.

returns to the ocean to eat. The dads can't eat during this time. If they drop the egg it will die, so hunting is out of the question. Males can lose 40 percent of their body weight. To conserve energy, they sleep most of the day and move very little. To help keep warm in temperatures that can easily go below minus 50 degrees Fahrenheit, the males huddle together. The warmest spot in the huddle is in the middle. The penguins all take turns being the one in the middle.

After all that waiting and careful balancing, the eggs finally hatch. Around that time, the moms return and find their mates. Like the Adelies, they listen for their mate's call. But unlike the Adelies, Emperor penguins usually don't choose the same mate year after year.

The chicks are covered in a soft gray down but they still need protection from the cold weather. The male moves the chick onto the female's feet and then heads off to sea to eat while she takes over parenting duties. If a mother doesn't return to the nest before the chick hatches, the father can produce a special secretion that is rich in protein and fat to keep the chick from starving for a day or two. After the males have had a chance to eat, they return to their family. From then on, the males and females take turns caring for the chicks until they are full grown and ready to be on their own. This happens in December, which is summer.

Flying in the Water

Adelies and Emperors are well adapted to their coldwater environments. Like their flying kin—birds—they have feathers. Penguins' feathers are small and tightly spaced. Feathers cover the entire body of a penguin except for its three-toed, webbed feet and beak. The Adelie even has feathers halfway down its beak to warm the air as it breathes in.

Penguins condition their feathers every day by rubbing oil on them. This oil comes from a special gland found on the lower part of a penguin's back. To spread the oil, the penguin reaches back with his beak, gets some oil on it, and then uses his beak to spread the oil around. The oil also helps form a watertight barrier.

Each year, penguins lose their feathers and new ones grow in. This is called **molting** and can take several weeks. While a penguin is molting, it can't eat because it can't swim; the icy water would be too dangerous without full feather protection.

These Birds Can Fly

Penguins are not the only kind of bird that lives in the Antarctic. There are 13 species of flying birds that nest and hunt on or near Antarctica. Most are seabirds, meaning they spend a lot of time flying over or near water. These include the skua (the pirates that like to steal penguin eggs), petrels, blue-eyed cormorant, fulmars, terns, and the wandering albatross. Most of the Antarctic birds leave the area during the winter months. The wandering albatross stays behind, though, and, like Emperor penguins, lays its eggs during the winter. Sheathbills are the only flying birds that live on the continent the whole year. They are land birds, which means they don't fly over water. Antarctic birds keep warm pretty much the same way penguins do. They have dense feathers and a layer of fat under their skin. They also fluff their feathers, which helps trap air and act as insulation.

Under the penguins' feathers is a soft, warm fur called down. And under their skin is a layer of fat, which helps insulate against the wind and cold. A penguin's feet are protected from the cold by its blood system, which doesn't allow the blood in the feet to get below the freezing point.

Penguins may not be able to fly in the air, but boy, can they fly in the water! Their bones, unlike the bones of most birds, are dense. This makes them almost neutrally buoyant, which means they neither sink nor float. On the surface, penguins paddle like a duck. But

did you know?
The Galapagos penguin lives near the equator, on the Galapagos Islands.

underwater—watch out! They look and act like torpedoes. Penguins usually swim around four to five miles per hour, but they can go up to speeds of nine miles per hour. They use their tails to steer. When they want to come out of the water to rest on a floe, penguins can propel themselves as high as six feet out of the water.

Penguins are also excellent divers. The Emperor penguin is the deepest diver of all. It can dive down as deep as 1,800 feet. This is six times deeper than a champion human diver (with no equipment) can go. Deep diving allows them to eat squid and crab along with small fish. Penguins don't have teeth. Instead, they have stiff spines on the roof of their mouths and on their tongues. These spines help keep prey from escaping from the mouth before the penguin can eat it.

Penguins don't have any land predators. This is because no other animals live on Antarctica! There are dangers, though. Attacking from the air, skua birds can steal an Adelie's egg or chick. Skuas aren't a problem for Emperors since they lay their eggs in such a remote and cold area. And in the water, penguins must watch out for leopard seals and killer whales. Early Antarctic explorers sometimes hunted penguins for food and oil. This is no longer allowed. Today, the biggest threat to penguins is global warming, which is affecting the fast ice and pack ice the penguins depend on. Pollution, especially oil spills, is another threat to penguins.

Despite laws to protect them, many species of penguins are close to being added to the endangered and threatened species lists.

More
Things to Try

- Adelie and Emperor penguins often have to walk hundreds of miles to get to food or their nesting site. How long would it take you to travel 200 miles? Attach a pedometer (a device to record how far you walk) to yourself and see how many steps or miles you can travel in one day.

- To get an idea of how hard it is for the Emperor penguin to hold its egg, place a ball between your ankles and try to walk.

- Watch the Academy Award–winning documentary "March of the Penguins," a movie about the Emperor penguin.

Make Your Own
Toboggan
with Wheels

Penguins glide across the Antarctic ice on their bellies in a move that's called tobogganing. You need snow to use a real toboggan, but here is way you can slide on your belly even if there is no ice or snow around. You'll be using tools for this project so ask an adult for help.

Supplies

* 16 half-inch screws for the coaster wheels
* screwdriver
* 4 coaster wheels, 1 inch in diameter, available at most hardware stores
* plywood, 1 foot by 2 feet by half-inch
* drill
* spray paint, any color (optional)

1 Using the screws and screwdriver, attach a coaster wheel in each corner of the plywood. You want the wheels about 1 inch in from each side. Use the drill to get the holes for the screws started. Note: Since you'll be lying on top of the board, it's very important that the tops of the screws don't poke through. If they do, use a metal file to smooth them down and then cover the spot with several pieces of duct tape. Spray paint the top of your toboggan if you'd like.

2 To toboggan like a penguin, find a smooth, flat surface. Carefully lay down on the board with your belly in the middle of the board. Your head and feet will be hanging off the board. Put your hands at your sides and hold on to the edges of the board. IMPORTANT: Keep your fingers away from the wheels at all times so they don't get pinched. Have someone give you a little push or use your toes or hands to push yourself forward!

Make Your Own
Neutrally Buoyant Cup

Penguins are nearly neutrally buoyant. This means they don't really sink or float in the water. In this experiment, you can make a cup neutrally buoyant.

1 Carefully poke the ends of the wire into the plastic cup, near the top on each side. Fold the ends of the wire so they don't slide out of the cup. Your cup should look like a pail with a wire handle. Bend the wire handle until it looks like a fat, upside down "U" with a flat bottom.

2 Turn the cup over (so the handle is pointing down) and use the marker to decorate your cup to look like a penguin.

3 Fill the plastic bottle with water to within an inch of the top. Put a few drops of dishwashing liquid into the water and gently stir it in with your fingers. This step is important because the soap helps break the water's surface tension and makes the cup sink more easily.

Supplies

* lightweight wire, 5 inches long
* plastic cup
* black permanent marker
* 2-liter plastic bottle, with the top third cut off and labels removed
* water
* liquid dishwashing soap
* paper clips
* small metal washers or nut bolts

4 Unfold a paperclip so it's "S" shaped. Slide a washer or nut bolt onto one end of it. Attach the other end to the plastic cup's handle. Place the cup (handle-side down) into the plastic bottle with water. Does the cup sink or float?

5 Keep adding paper clips with washers or nut bolt weights. Can you get the cup to become neutrally buoyant? In other words, can you get the cup to a point where it neither goes up or down in the water? You may need to add paperclips without the washers or even cut the paperclips into small pieces to get the weight just right.

Ocean Animals
Seals, Walruses, and Whales

Polar bears and penguins aren't the only animals well adapted to the harsh weather of the polar region. There are many other animals who thrive in the icy waters and dark winters. Some of these animals are small. Some are very large. Some are cute and cuddly, and some are most definitely *not* cute and cuddly!

Seals

Seals come in all sizes, though they all have the same, basic, rounded shape. Some have skin and hair. Others have hair-like fur. They are **pinnipeds**, which means they are aquatic animals who use flippers to swim and move on land. There are at least a half dozen species of seals that live in the Arctic. These include the harp seal, hooded seal, ringed seal, bearded seal, spotted seal, and ribbon seal. The ringed seal is the most common.

Ringed seals are the smallest species of seal. They have a silvery pelt that has dark spots with white rings. The rings are how they got their name.

words to know

pennipeds: aquatic animals that use flippers to swim or move on land. The word means "wing-footed."

haul out: to climb out of the water.

air hole: a hole made in the ice by animals that must come up to breath.

They can grow to 4 or 5 feet long and weigh between 110 and 150 pounds. A thick layer of blubber helps keep them warm. Like all seals, ringed seals spend most of the their time in the water. But they do **haul out**, or climb out, to rest, mate, give birth, and nurse their pups.

Because ringed seals are mammals, they breathe air. They make **air holes** in the ice with their teeth. Sometimes, these air holes go through over six feet of ice! These air holes must be kept open all winter long, which means they have to be cleared of new ice frequently. Seals come up to breathe every 5 to 15 minutes. When they are using their air holes, seals must be very careful. Polar bears love to lie next to an air hole and wait for a tasty seal snack to pop up.

Mother seals hollow out a den in the ice to give birth and nurse. But even inside their dens, moms and their pups aren't safe from polar bears. Polar bears can smell them under the ice and will pounce on the roof of the den until it breaks. Fortunately, the mother seal and her pups can escape through a hole at the bottom of the den back into the ocean where they can feed on things like fish, shrimp, and squid.

There are hundreds of thousands of seals in the Arctic, but there are even more in the Antarctic. All of them are interesting, but some are downright peculiar! Take the elephant seal. The elephant seal is the largest species of seal in the Antarctic. Males (called bulls) can grow up to 13 feet long and up to 4,500 pounds. That's almost as long and as heavy as a small minivan!

Did you know?
Leopard seals will even attack humans who are standing along the edge of the ice!)

Elephant seals get their name from their large nose that looks kind of like an elephant's trunk. Or how about the crabeater? This seal doesn't even eat crab; it eats krill by sucking them through its sieve-like teeth. And how about the meanest, scariest looking seal of all—the leopard seal.

Named for the dark spots on its coat, the leopard seal is a slender seal measuring around 13 feet and weighing 1,000 pounds. With their long, flexible necks, wide mouth, and sharp teeth, they look as if they belong back in the time of dinosaurs. Leopard seals are great swimmers, and love to hunt penguins along the edge of the ice. Its only natural predator is the orca, or killer whale.

Walruses

Walruses are close relatives of seals. They only live in the Northern Hemisphere and are the largest pinniped in the Arctic. They don't stay there during the winter, though. Like many seals, they migrate to warmer waters. Male walruses, called bulls, are usually between 10 and 12 feet long and can weigh up to 3,700 pounds—about the size of a small car! Females (cows) are a bit smaller, weighing up to 2,700 pounds. Walruses' blob-like bodies are covered with a very thick skin and stiff hairs. A layer of blubber helps protect them from the cold. Unlike other pinnipeds who drag their back legs, walruses can walk on all four of their flippers.

What makes walruses really stand out isn't their size or the way they walk—it's their ivory tusks. A walruses' tusk is actually a tooth. A cow's tusk can be two feet long. A bull's tusk can be up to four feet long.

did you know?
A walrus can eat as many as 1,000 clams at one meal.

Bulls use their tusk to fight off other bulls during mating season, and both male and females use it to make air holes in the ice and to pull themselves up onto the ice to rest.

Tusks are not used for hunting. In fact, they get in the way of eating since they keep the walrus from being able to get to food below it. To find food, walruses use their long whiskers to feel around. Then, they blow on the food to get it to move up to a place where they can eat it. Walruses eat things like snail, crabs, and shrimp.

Walruses are social animals. They like to hang out together in large herds on the ice or rocky coasts along the Arctic Circle. Like their cousins the seals, walruses make plenty of noise above and below water. They bark, whoop, scream, tap, and click. These sounds are "sung" in short and long patterns and are used to attract mates. They are kind of like the songs that whales sing.

Whales

Many species of whale visit the Arctic waters. These include the narwhal, beluga, bowhead, and humpback whales. Whales are not fish. They are marine mammals. Many people probably recognize the playful, white beluga, the jumping humpback, and the bowhead with its extra large mouth. But are you familiar with the narwhal?

Narwhals spend all their time in the cold Arctic waters. Like other whale species, narwhals have a thick layer of blubber that keeps them warm. Males can be 20 feet long and weigh 3,500 pounds. What makes narwhals special is that the males have a long, spiral tooth that extends from their face. It makes them look like some kind of ocean unicorn! In fact, narwhals are even called the unicorn of the sea. This tooth is between six and nine feet long. Some females have the tooth, too, but it's much shorter than the males'.

Ever since men first saw narwhals, they considered them mysterious. Many ancient people thought the narwhal's tooth had magical powers. For example, legend says that it was a remedy for poison. Queens have paid a handsome sum for a narwhal's tooth. They were often used for decoration in the palace or to make royal scepters.

But the real use of the tooth has been a bit of a mystery. Scientists have many theories. One is that the tooth is used for defense. Another is that it's used to show off to females. Or perhaps it's used to communicate. Recently, researchers have discovered that the tooth is unlike any other tooth known to us. It is very strong and yet very flexible. It has a bundle of nerves running down its middle. Some experts believe these things may mean the tooth is some kind of super sensor the narwhal uses to determine the water's temperature, pressure, and salt level, which may help the narwhal find certain kinds of fish for food.

did you know?
One blue whale can eat four tons of krill a day. That's roughly 40 million krill.

Blue whales live all over the world but like to migrate to the polar regions during the spring and summer. Blue whales are the largest animals ever to live on Earth; they're even bigger than any known dinosaur. Females are usually bigger than males. They can grow to be 100 feet long (that's almost as long as three school buses lined up) and weigh 100 tons. Its heart is so large that a human could sit inside its chambers.

The Tiniest Sea Creatures

Orcas may be at the top of the food chain, but what's at the bottom? The answer is zooplankton and phytoplankton.

Phytoplankton is small plant life. Algae is a good example. Algae does very well in the Arctic and Antarctic because the cold water temperatures can hold gases (for instance, carbon dioxide) that the plant needs to survive. Algae also does well because the ice traps it inside tiny spaces and channels and thus allows the sun to reach it.

Zooplankton, or tiny animal life, eats the phytoplankton. Krill is a vital zooplankton in the polar regions. Krill is a pinkish, shrimp-like creature with long antennae and five pairs of legs for swimming. They are generally between one and two inches long. Krill swim together in large groups called swarms, or clouds. Sometimes, a swarm is so big that the ocean looks pink! Because so many fish and whales eat them, krill are considered a keystone species. Keystone species are ones that many other species rely on to survive.

Like all whales, blue whales come up for air and breathe through a special hole on the back of their heads called a blowhole. But unlike most whales, blues have two blowholes instead of one.

Blue whales are a kind of baleen whale. **Baleen plates** are sections of long, closely spaced, fringe-like material that hangs from a whale's jaw.

did you know?
Blue whales are the loudest of all whales; their call is louder than the sound a jet engine makes.

To eat, a blue whale open its mouth wide, swallows a large amount of water, and then squeezes the water through its 800 baleen plates. It's kind of like when you spit water through your teeth. The water is pushed out and the food is trapped behind. Blue whales eat a shrimp-like animal called **krill**. Not surprisingly, such a large whale needs to eat a lot.

Besides baleen whales, there are also toothed whales. A familiar toothed whale in the Arctic and Antarctic is the Orca, or killer whale. Orcas are the large black and white whales that are popular at aquarium shows.

words to know

baleen plates: sections of long, fringe-like material that hangs from a whale's jaw and helps it eat.
krill: a small, shrimp-like creature.
pod: a group of whales.

Males are about 30 feet long and weigh eight tons. Though they look friendly enough, they are at the top of the ocean's food chain. With their speed in the water (about 25 knots) and 50 three-inch long teeth, they can eat just about anything they want! Fish, seals, birds, other whales, squid, and plankton are all included in their diet.

Orcas are very social creatures and travel together in large groups called **pods**. These pods typically have around 50 members. To communicate, Orcas make clicks, squeaks, pops, and whistles. Each pod has a different accent, or dialect. A pod uses the accent to recognize each other from other groups.

More Things to Try

- The scientific name of the blue whale is Balsenoptera musculus, which means "mouse-like finned whale." It was probably a joke because of the whale's unusually large size. Research what your own name means, or come up with a nickname that represents the opposite of who you are.

- Listen to a humpback whale's song. Here's a place to try: http://dsc.discovery.com/convergence/blueplanet/sounds/sounds.html

Make Your Own
Narwhal Tusk

Narwhal tusks are the only animal tusks that are straight. Perhaps this is one reason why they're supposed to have mystical qualities. Here is a fun and easy way to make your own scale model of a narwhal tusk. If you'd like to make the tusk life-size, simply double the materials and connect two sections together using the plaster cloth.

Supplies

* lots of newspaper
* masking tape
* roll of jute string or small craft rope
* scissors
* 2 rolls of plaster cloth, sometimes called plaster gauze (found near the plaster of Paris in many craft stores; Rigid Wrap is one brand name)
* medium-sized container of water
* ivory spray paint or ivory craft paint

1 Unfold your newspaper and spread some of the single sheets around your work area. Open the double spreads. Make one stack of 10 double pages and one stack of five double pages.

2 Start with the stack of 10 pages. Roll the stack lengthwise into a tight paper log that is approximately 2 feet long. Use a few pieces of masking tape to keep the paper log from unrolling.

3 Fold the stack of five double pages width-wise. Roll them together into a tight paper roll that is approximately 1 foot long. Use a few pieces of masking tape to keep the paper log together. Tape the two pieces together to form a 3-foot-long paper log.

4 Next, tape the end of the jute string at one end of the paper log. Begin wrapping the jute around the paper in a spiral fashion. There should be about an inch between the lines. When you reach the other end of the paper log, cut the jute and tape it down. The jute is what will help create the spiral formation that is typical of narwhals' tusks.

5 Cut the plaster cloth into strips that are about 6 inches long. If you want to make them longer, you can. Just choose a length that is easy for you to work with. Dip a strip into the water. Beginning at one end, wrap the wet plaster cloth around the paper log and jute in a spiral fashion. Continue adding plaster cloth until the whole "tusk" is covered. Use wet fingers to smooth out the cloth. Note: don't add more than three layers or you won't be able to see the spiral.

6 Narwhal tusks are slightly pointed at the top. Add a point to your tusk by molding some plaster cloth. You can also use some foil or a bit of extra newspaper to form a point at one end. Just cover it with plaster cloth as well.

7 Let the tusk dry completely. This may take several days. Once the tusk is dry, paint it following the directions on the paint bottle or spray can. Now, you have a tusk that is about half the size of a real narwhal's tusk!

Exploring
the Polar Region

People have always had a fascination with the top and bottom of the world. The challenge to go there—and be the first—lured many, especially in the early 1900s. In fact, this time period is usually referred to as the Heroic Age of Arctic/Antarctic Exploration. Unfortunately, many of the earliest attempts were ill fated. Countless teams of men that headed off to find glory were simply never heard from ever again.

There are many challenges with polar exploration. First and foremost is the constant and brutal cold. Unlike the Inuit who lived there all their lives, early Arctic explorers were not accustomed to the weather. Though they brought warm clothes, early explorers were seldom prepared to deal with frostbite and **hypothermia**. Sunburn is also a serious problem because the sun's rays reflect off the snow and ice.

Navigating across vast plains of ice that looks the same in all directions is difficult. Ships got stuck in the crushing ice. Early explorers often lacked enough fuel to keep warm, run their ship, and melt ice for drinking water. Explorers suffered from **scurvy** because they didn't carry fresh fruit and lead poisoning from

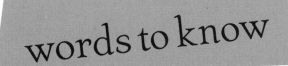

words to know

hypothermia: when the body's temperature falls below 95 degrees.

scurvy: a serious illness caused by a lack of vitamin C in someone's diet. It's common in sailors and others who go a long time without fresh fruit.

badly canned food. They also didn't use sled dogs, which could carry heavy equipment and make travel over the ice much easier.

Arctic Disaster

One of the most famous Arctic expeditions is known not for its success but for its failure! This is the expedition led by Sir John Franklin.

John Franklin was an officer in England's Royal Navy. He was an experienced Arctic explorer when he embarked on a journey to discover the Northwest Passage. This is a route through the Arctic Ocean to connect the Atlantic and Pacific Oceans. With a crew of about 125 on two ships, *Erebus* and *Terror,* Franklin set sail in early 1845. The boats and crew were last spotted near an iceberg in late June.

Franklin's wife, Jane, began a campaign to convince American and British teams to search for her missing husband and crew. The public became fascinated with the mystery: *What happened to the ships? Were Franklin and his crew still alive?* Newspapers across the world carried the story. Over 40 search parties were sent out between 1848 and 1859. These ships and their crews helped chart previously unknown areas and discovered valuable information about the Arctic.

So what *did* happen to Franklin and his crew? An 1859 expedition found clues such as skeletons and clothes. They also found a letter, hidden under a pile of rocks, which said the ships had become stuck in the ice. After Franklin died on June 11, 1847, the crew set off on foot for a navy post about 900 miles away. They never made it.

Compass Doesn't Work? Hmmmm...

Scottish explorer James Clark Ross was the first person to find the Magnetic North Pole. He did this in 1831 while aboard the *Victory*. The boat had become stuck in the ice. While the crew waited for the ice to melt, Ross noticed that's the ship's compass was acting strangely. So he began looking for, and eventually found, the Magnetic North Pole. This discovery led the British government to support an expedition to find the Magnetic South Pole. Ross Island, Ross Sea, and the Ross Ice Shelf in Antarctica are named for James Clark Ross.

The Race to the North Pole

Of course, one of the biggest prizes of early Arctic exploration was to reach the North Pole first. Unlike those who searched for the Northwest Passage in ships, expedition teams heading to the North Pole would have to travel by dog sled.

Accidentally First

Matthew Hensen was an African-American who accompanied Robert Peary on many of his expeditions. This includes the one in 1909, when Peary claims to have reached the North Pole. Hensen was a skilled navigator and could speak the Inuit language. According to reports, Peary sent Hensen and some Inuit men ahead to scout out the right location on April 6. Approximately an hour ahead of Peary, Hensen overshot the estimated distance. This means that if Peary's claims are to be believed, Hensen accidentally became the first, non-Inuit man to reach the North Pole! When Peary caught up, Hensen reportedly said, "I think I'm the first man to sit on top of the world." As you can imagine, Peary was not happy about this. But because he was the expedition leader, Peary received the full credit for being first. Prejudice against African-Americans kept Hensen from getting the recognition he deserved until much later.

Many explorers set out for the North Pole, only to turn back or perish. By 1909, though, two men each claimed to have reached it by dogsled. These men were Dr. Frederick Cook and Robert Peary. The question of who reached it first—or if they had, in fact, reached it at all—was hotly debated for many years.

Dr. Cook was an American doctor. He had accompanied a couple of expedition teams before deciding to claim the North Pole. Supposedly, Cook and his team set off in February 1908. The team claims to have reached their goal on April 1, 1908. But it wasn't until May of 1909 that he reached a place where he could share his news. This might seem strange, but you have to remember there were no such things as the Internet, television, or cell phones back then. And the radios they did have couldn't transmit that far.

Cook was celebrating his big success when he heard some startling news: another American explorer

named Robert Peary claimed to have reached the North Pole, too. Peary supposedly left with his team in February 1908 too and reached the North Pole on April 6, 1909. It appeared that Peary had been second to reach the goal. But there was more! Peary claimed that Cook was lying. He said there was no evidence at the North Pole that Cook had been there. As you can imagine, this did not go over well with Cook, who said the moving ice must have taken the evidence.

During the following years, Cook and Peary and their supporters feuded. Reaching the North Pole was such a huge feat; it meant fame and money. It's no surprise neither side would budge on its claims to be the first to stand on top of the world. Though each man still has his supporters,

did you know?
In 1958, the U.S.S. Nautilus became the first submarine to reach the North Pole by going under the ice.

modern examination of the evidence discredits both men. Or maybe that should be the *lack* of evidence; neither Cook nor Peary ever produced the **logbooks** that might prove their claims. Many experts agree, however, that between the two men Peary probably got the closest.

The claim to have been the first to fly over the North Pole was also controversial. On May 9, 1926, U.S. Navy pilots Richard Byrd and Floyd Bennet claimed to be the first to reach the North Pole by aircraft. Doubts surfaced about the claim,

words to know

logbook: a notebook or journal that sailors, pilots, and other explorers use to record daily details about their travels.

Adventure, Fame and Business too

Of course, adventure and fame were not the only reasons people explored the polar regions. In the Arctic, at least, there was an important economic reason: countries were looking for quicker shipping routes through oceans so they could import and export more goods. These passages, or routes, are the Northwest Passage and the Northeast Passage. The Northwest Passage is the route between the Atlantic and Pacific Oceans that follows along the coasts of Canada and Alaska. It was first sailed by Roald Amundsen between 1903 and 1906. The Northeast Passage is the route that connects the Atlantic and Pacific Oceans travelimg along the coasts of Scandinavia and Russia. It was first sailed by a Swede named Nils Adolf Erik Nordenskiold between 1878 and 1879.

though, because some felt that Byrd and Bennet couldn't possibly have reached the North Pole in the amount of time they said they did. Years later, in the 1950s, a writer said Bennet confessed that he and Byrd didn't make it. Furthermore, scholars who have studied the flight log say the pair's notes suggest they had to turn back because of engine trouble before reaching their goal. Both sides—those who support Byrd's claim and those who don't—continue to debate the issue today. Byrd later went on to become an important Antarctic explorer.

So just who claimed to reach the North Pole and *could prove it?* That would be the men aboard the airship called the *Norge.* Carefully documenting their voyage, the crew of the hydrogen-filled *Norge* floated over the North Pole on May 12, 1926. This was just three days after Byrd said he had done it! Inside the *Norge* were explorers Umberto Nobile, Roald Amundsen, and Lincoln Ellsworth. To celebrate, the three men and their crew dropped poles with flags from their countries (Italy, Norway, and America, respectfully) onto the North Pole's ice.

Explorer, Aviator, Mapmaker: The Extraordinary Richard Byrd

Though his flight to the North Pole was controversial, Admiral Richard Byrd played a key role in exploring Antarctica. In 1928, after raising money using his North Pole fame, Byrd led an expedition to the continent. Byrd set up a large camp, which he nicknamed "Little America." From there, Byrd and his crew began exploring Antarctica by air. He even followed Amundsen's route across the continent and over the South Pole by plane. In later years, Byrd made two more significant expeditions. In 1933, he spent the winter alone in a tiny hut in order to study the weather. He nearly died from carbon monoxide poisoning when the chimney was blocked by snow. And in 1946, Byrd led the largest Antarctic expedition that had ever been put together, called Operation Highjump, which helped map over 1.5 million square miles of the continent.

The Race to the South Pole

Roald Amundsen was a Norwegian explorer and the first person to sail through the Northwest Passage. He had set his sights on reaching the North Pole first. But once he heard that people were claiming they'd done it, he quickly—and quietly—changed his goal. He decided to try to become the first person to reach the South Pole. He knew others would also try, including a British explorer named Robert Scott.

In August 1910, Amundsen and his crew of about 20 men began their quest. The trip was rough. First, they had to break through the sea's choking ice and then travel over the icy land using dogsleds. Frostbite, sunburn, dangerous glaciers, and sheer boredom plagued the men. But on December 15, 1911, Amundsen and a few members of his crew reached the South Pole.

While there, Amundsen and his men took plenty of notes and verified their navigations. They even walked several miles in all directions just to make sure they could safely claim they had reached the South Pole. Afterwards, the team set up a tent. Amundsen left a letter inside the tent addressed to the King of Norway—and a note asking Scott to deliver it!

Scott and four members of his party reached the South Pole a month later. (The rest of the group stayed behind on Ross Island.) The group was low on food and exhausted from carrying all their supplies. Scott had brought ponies instead of sled dogs, and the ponies didn't work out very well. Finding the note from Amundsen was very disappointing. Unfortunately, the return trip proved disastrous for Scott and his men. The group battled brutal weather and a lack of food. Two of the five soon died. A terrible blizzard eventually trapped Scott and the other two men inside their tent. They were only 11 miles from a food supply but just couldn't get there.

In November, 1912, a search party found the bodies of Scott and his friends frozen in the tent. The search party also found Scott's diary. The last entry read in part:

"*Every day we have been ready to start for our depot 11 miles away, but outside the door of the tent it remains a scene of whirling drift. I do not think we can hope for any better things now. We shall stick it out to the end, but we are getting weaker, of course, and the end cannot be far. It seems a pity, but I do not think I can write more.*"

Shackleton's Attempt to Cross Antarctica

Like the Arctic, the Antarctic also had a famous disaster. But this one has a happier ending. Ernest Shackleton was an Irish explorer. He had already been to the Antarctic a couple of times when he decided he wanted to be the first to travel across the continent. Unlike other expedition leaders, Shackleton listened to the advice of whalers and packed extra fuel. He consulted nutritionists and took plenty of good food, including vegetables, powdered milk, sugar, and canned meats. He also packed special treats such as liquor, cocoa, live pigs, and tobacco. To entertain and care for his crew, Shackleton brought weapons, science and photography equipment, radios, fuel, tents, matches, lanterns, and recreational items such as mini billiards, books, board games, and instruments.

In August, 1914, Shackleton and his crew of 28 set sail on the *Endurance* for Antarctica. Unfortunately, the *Endurance* became stuck far from land in the Weddell Sea's ice, and then the ice crushed the ship and it sank. Luckily the crew was able to save their supplies and set up camp on the ice. Stranded for many months, the crew did their best to keep themselves entertained. They played soccer and board games, listened to music, put on plays, played practical jokes on each other, and held dog races. They even decorated the sled dogs' houses, dubbed "dogloos" because they were made with blocks of ice.

More
Things to Try

- Shackleton's exciting tale of survival and adventure is documented in books and movies. One excellent account is the book *Shipwreck at the Bottom of the World* by Jennifer Armstrong.

- Arctic and Antarctic expeditions often carried props so the men could put on plays for each other. Create your own prop box. You can fill it with things like old clothes, hats, shoes, jewelry, old telephones, or anything else you might think would be fun to have.

Once the ice began to break up, around late December 1915, the crew headed for land. It wasn't an easy trip. They had to carry all their supplies and drag their lifeboats over the ice when they couldn't sail. It took them until April to make it to land, a remote island called Elephant Island. Unfortunately, if there were to be any hope of rescue, they would have to go for help. And that's just what they did: Shackleton and five other men sailed in a lifeboat across 800 miles of cold and turbulent ocean to a whaling station. They sent a ship back for the remaining men, although it took until August to reach them. Unbelievably, every single man survived.

Women at the Poles

Women were not part of the early Arctic and Antarctic explorations. Society considered women incapable of enduring the hardships of polar travel. But a few brave women battled prejudice along with the cold over the years. In 1935, Caroline Mikkelsen, the wife of a Norwegian whaler, became the first woman to step foot on the continent of Antarctica. And in 1955, an American named Louise Arner Boyd became the first woman to fly over the North Pole. Boyd had been interested in the Arctic for most of her life and was even nicknamed the "ice woman." She was 67 at the time of her historic flight!

On January 14, 1993, the first women to reach the South Pole by foot (or, more accurately, by ski) were part of a four-women American team. Led by Arctic explorer Ann Bancroft, the team also included Sunniva Sorby, Sue Giller, and Anne Dal Vera. The women kept journals and documented their 67-day journey in order to help teach children about Antarctica. They wanted to encourage people of all ages to live their dreams.

As the group of women approached the South Pole, workers at the nearby station cheered the historic event. Describing the moment, Ann wrote, "We tossed our video camera to someone and touched the Pole together."

Make Your Own
Sun Goggles

The goggles that early polar explorers used weren't like the plastic snow goggles we have today. They were made out of leather, and while they may have looked strange, they were necessary to help prevent sun blindness.

1 Use the scissors to round the corners of the piece of craft foam or leather. Hold the piece of foam up to your face so that it covers your eyes. Have someone use the pen to make a mark on the foam where your eyes are. Be very careful not to push too hard with the pen so you don't hurt your eyes!

2 Next, use the scissors to cut eye slits in the foam where the pen marks are. The slits shouldn't be ovals. They should be long, thin lines just big enough to see through.

3 Punch holes in each of the four, rounded corners. Tie one end of a leather cord through each hole.

4 Now, your polar-style sun goggles are ready to go. To put them on, tie the two top cords together behind your head. Next, tie the two bottom cords together.

Supplies

* craft foam or a piece of leather, 8 inches by 2 inches
* scissors
* marker or pen
* hole punch
* 4 pieces of leather cord, each 12 inches long (leather shoelaces work well, too)

Make Your Own
"Dogloo"

Shackelton's crew spent many hours decorating their dogs' ice houses just for fun. They called them "dogloos" and gave them fancy roofs and even porches! The dogs didn't appreciate the effort, though. They usually slept outside.

1 In the mixing bowl, soak the shredded crêpe paper in the warm water for several hours or until the paper is very soft.

2 Drain off any extra water and sprinkle in most of the flour. Use your hands to knead the mixture together. After the dough is mixed, place it on a piece of waxed paper and sprinkle in the rest of the flour. Knead the dough until it is soft and feels like pie crust. Set the dough aside for a moment.

3 Turn the small, plastic container over and cut an arched opening in one side. This will be your dogloo's "door." The container should now look kind of like a plastic cave. Place the container upside down on another piece of waxed paper.

Supplies

* mixing bowl
* 1 to 2 cups shredded, white crêpe paper
* 1 to 2 cups of warm water
* $3/4$ cup all-purpose flour
* waxed paper
* small, plastic container
* scissors
* markers

4 Use the white dough to cover the plastic container and create a dogloo. Get creative! Maybe your dogloo can have a steeple or a chimney. Maybe it can have fake windows and a pyramid-shaped roof or even a satellite dish!

5 You can also use the dough to create a miniature sled dog, if you'd like. When you're done, allow your dog and dogloo to dry for several days. When the dough is hard, you can use markers to decorate the dog.

Living
in the Arctic

It may be hard to believe, but people have lived in the Arctic region for thousands of years. Though they live in many places and speak different languages, these people have plenty in common. Mainly, they have all adapted to life in the cold and harsh climate. They are proud of where they live, and work hard to keep their histories and traditions alive.

The native people who live in the Arctic tundra, call themselves **Inuit**, which means "the people." Early European explorers called the native people "Eskimos," which means "eaters of raw meat." But many Inuit people find that name offensive. The Inuit are the native group in the Arctic that people are probably most familiar with.

The Inuit

The Inuit have been around for about 5,000 years. Early Inuit divided themselves into small groups of extended families and were nomadic, which means they moved from place to place. In the summer, they lived along the coasts, fishing, hunting, and eating stored food to survive. In the winter, they left their partially buried sod houses or animal skin tents and went out on the ice. There, they built igloos. **Igloos** are dome-shaped dwellings made out of cut blocks of snow. Though they are made of ice, igloos are surprisingly warm. This is because the snow acts as an insulator. It takes about an hour or two to make a comfortably sized igloo. Inside, oil lamps provide light and extra warmth. Small holes cut into the blocks of snow allow smoke from the lamp and cooking fires to escape.

Out on the ice, the Inuit used spears and harpoons to hunt polar bears, whales, and seals. Like polar bears, the Inuit learned to wait patiently for seals by their air holes. The Inuit believed that all animals and other living things had spirits. They respected the animals they hunted by using every part of them that they could. They used animals and their bones for food, clothing, tools, weapons, building, and art materials. The Inuit also respected animals by following certain hunting rituals. For example, they didn't hunt animals during their mating season.

words to know

Inuit: the native people who live in the Arctic tundra, Northern Canada, Russia, Greenland, and Alaska.

igloo: a temporary, Inuit dwelling made out of blocks of snow.

words to know

umiaks: big, rowboat-like boats that the Inuit used to hunt whales and to move their families.

Little Ice Age: a period of time that began about 700 years ago when the temperatures in the Northern Hemisphere began to cool down.

Sami: the native people who live in Sweden, Norway, Finland, and the Kola Peninsula of Russia.

Chukchi: the native people of the northeasternmost part of Siberia.

shaman: a wise leader, who native people believe has special powers and can connect to the spiritual world.

Hunting in snow and ice could be difficult since there were no landmarks. To keep from getting lost, the Inuit made rock markers called Inuksuit. With rock "heads" and outstretched "arms," these formations often resembled rock people!

The Inuit wore parkas (long coats), and pants made of caribou fur to keep warm. Caribou fur is one of the warmest kinds of material there is. It's even warmer than most manmade material. The parkas had fur-lined hoods that pulled together so only a tiny part of a person's face showed. This helped the wearer keep warm. And mittens were permanently attached to the end of the parka's sleeves. They wore boots made of caribou fur when on land. When they were out on the ice or sailing in the ocean, they wore boots called kamiks. Kamiks were made of sealskin, which was waterproof.

Inuits also used sealskin to make kayaks. Kayaks are long, single person boats that are completely enclosed except where the person paddling the craft sits. Inuits used kayaks to hunt seal. They used bigger boats called **umiaks** to hunt whale. Umiaks were kind of like rowboats made of skin and wood

Inuit Language

Inuit people share the same basic language. It is called Inuktitut. There are many, many different dialects, though. Dialects are a certain style or way of speaking a language. Their writing language, called Syllabics, uses symbols to stand for the syllables of words.

Speaking of words, there is a rumor that the Inuit have 100 different words or phrases for snow. This isn't true. This myth began many years ago when someone wrote about how the Inuit have four different root words for snow. The story (pardon the pun) snowballed from there. Someone assumed this meant that each kind of snow must have its own name. Pretty soon, people were creating lists of "snow words" and even making up words. The truth is, the Inuit have around the same number of words for types of snow as the English language does.

frames. Inuits also used umiaks to move their families. Other modes of transportation included snowshoes, dogsleds, and skis. To make walking on slippery ice easier, Inuits invented crampons. Crampons are spiked plates you can attach to your boot.

About 700 years ago, the Arctic experienced a period of time when temperatures cooled down. During this time, called the **Little Ice Age,** the Inuit began to struggle. The colder weather meant that ice closed off leads, which are the paths between ice floes. Whales couldn't migrate to where the Inuit lived. On top of that, Europeans began hunting whales, which meant there were fewer whales for Inuit to hunt. Some Inuits moved to other areas further south and began hunting land animals for fur. As more and more outsiders also settled in these areas, the Inuit began to lose their culture. And while some of the things the outsiders brought were good (for example, iron for tools), other things were not so

A Whale of a Good Time

Whale hunts are a tradition the Inuit sometimes still continue. Men in umiaks work together to harpoon a whale. The men then bring the whale back to the community for a celebration. Then the whale is divided up among all the people. The Inuit then make muktuk. Muktuk is whale blubber with skin. First, the people cut the whale blubber into thin pink and black strips. Next, the pieces are boiled or left to dry for a week. Boiled pieces are soft, but the raw pieces are chewy.

good, namely diseases. The Inuit weren't immune to things like dysentery and the flu and many of them died. In order to survive, many Inuit moved into government-established settlements.

During the 1960s and 1970s, Inuit and other native groups organized and started to demand representation and rights to their native land. In Canada, Inuit tribes joined together and agreed to a land settlement from the Canadian government. In the early 1990s, Canada turned over around 130,000 square miles of land that eventually lead to the creation of a new territory. This new territory, officially established in 1999, is called Nunavut, which means "our land."

Today, many Inuits mix tradition with modern ways. Most live in wooden houses and go to work or school. Inuit children continue to play and sing traditional songs but also enjoy rock music and video games. Some Inuits wear modern clothes, while others prefer kamiks and caribou mittens. Though they may rely on hunting for a lot of their food, they also go to grocery stores. But instead of dogsleds, they take snowmobiles to get there! Because of their understanding of

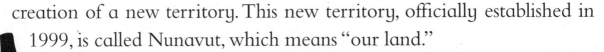

and longtime ties to the land, many Inuit are also helping scientists to track changes in the Arctic ice and wildlife.

The Sami and Chukchi

There are many, many tribes of native people living in the Arctic region. Besides the Inuit, two of the biggest and most well-known groups are the **Sami** and **Chukchi.** The Sami, or Lapps, are the native people who live in Sweden, Norway, Finland, and the Kola Peninsula of Russia. Because this region is collectively called Lapland, the Sami are also known as Laplanders, although some find this name offensive.

Like the Inuit, they have been around for a long time, about 4,000 years. The early Sami were also nomadic and believed all things in nature had a spirit. They survived by fishing and trapping animals for food and fur. But they were mainly known for herding and breeding reindeer. When their herd moved, they moved as well. Instead of living in an igloo, they had tents called lavvus. These were made of wooden poles and animal skins and looked like flattened out teepees. Lavvus were built low to the ground to handle the cold, fast winds of the Arctic. Like the Inuit, the Sami kept warm by wearing thick parkas made from reindeer skin and fur.

The Chukchi are the native people of the northeasternmost part of Siberia, divided into two groups. The members of one group lived along the coasts

Spiritual Leaders

The Inuit, Sami, and Chukchi don't really have organized religions. But they all have special leaders called **shamans**, or angakoks. They believe shamans have supernatural powers that can connect to the spiritual world. Shamans are more than just wise, spiritual leaders, though. They often act as healers and miracle workers who can predict, or even control, weather or future events.

as fisherman and fur traders. The members of the other group were nomadic, reindeer herders. Their tents were called yarangas. These tents were made of reindeer skin and were easy to move from place to place. Today, most Chukchi (like Sami) live in towns with modern facilities. There are some Chukchi, though, that continue to follow the traditional way of life and herd reindeer across the tundra.

Like the Inuit, the Sami and Chukchi have struggled in modern history. Outsiders moved in and brought diseases that they weren't immune to. Those same outsiders took control of their land and tried to destroy their cultures. Laws forbade the Sami and Chukchi to speak their native languages. In recent years, however, both the Sami and Chukchi have organized themselves to stand up for their rights and to regain control of their native lands.

More Things to Try

- Listen to some Inuktitut phrases at http://www.ainc-inac.gc.ca/ks/5020_e.html.

- See how many different "snow" words or words with the root word "snow" you can think of. Here are just a few: flurries, blizzard, ice, snowman, and snowmobile.

Play an **Inuit Game**

The Arctic winters are cold, long, and dark. To entertain themselves, Inuit children played games. Because the Inuit were nomadic, their games usually didn't require much equipment. This meant fewer things to move! Often, games were designed to help improve strength and endurance, things that were necessary to survive in the Arctic. Here are two very simple, traditional games to try. Many Inuit children still play these games today.

Supplies
❄ two players
❄ strong stick about 3 feet long, such as an old broom handle

Thong Pull (also called Ac Sa Raq)

Players should sit on the floor facing each with each player's legs straight out in front and touching the other player's feet. Opponents should hold onto the stick. One person's hands should be between the other player's hands. You can toss a coin to see who gets to decide to put his or her hands on the outside, or just take turns.

When you and the other player are ready, the two of you can begin pulling the stick while keeping your legs straight. The object of the game is to pull your opponent's bottom off the ground *or* get him or her to let go of the stick. Play the best out of three games to find the winner.

Back to Back

To begin, you and your partner should sit on the floor, back to back. Knees should be bent and both feet flat on the floor. Everybody's hands should be at their sides and flat on the floor, too. Count to three together and then say, "Go." Use your legs and backs to push against each other. The object of the game is to try to push your opponent across a designated line or out of the playing area. Once play has started, hands and feet can come off the floor to help push or balance. Bottoms should not lift more than a few inches off the ground, though.

Make Your Own
Soapstone Carving

Supplies

❊ rectangular bar of soap, new. Ivory soap works well because it's softer than other soaps.

❊ pencil or pen

❊ paring knife or other carving tools. Carving tools can be found at any craft store in the wood-working section.

❊ waxed paper

The Inuit often carved beautiful and elaborate models, sculptures, and masks out of bone, ivory, and animal antlers. Today, Inuit artists use soapstone (a soft, soapy feeling rock) as well. Their art is highly prized by collectors and tourists. Here's an easy and fun way to make your own model even if you don't have any soapstone handy. You'll be using a paring knife, so ask an adult for help.

1 Spread a piece of waxed paper over your work area.

2 Use the pencil to sketch out a simple design on the top of the soap. Traditional Inuit designs include polar bears, seals, whales, sleds, and people wearing parkas.

3 Next, use the paring knife to carefully carve your soap into the desired design. When you're done, you can smooth any rough edges by dipping your fingers in water and gently running them over the soap.

4 The Inuit believed in using every piece of an animal or a material, so recycle the extra bits of soap. Collect the extra pieces, add a small amount of water, and mold them into another bar of soap or decorative design to use in the bathroom or kitchen.

Make Your Own
Miniature Inuksuk

An inuksuk is an Inuit trail marker. When you are looking for stones for this project, try to find ones that are fairly flat and smooth. They will balance on top of each other better. You'll need a rounded stone for the Inuksuk's "head" though. If you can't find any rocks near your house, you can also use smooth river rocks, which can often be found in craft stores in the floral department.

Supplies

✳ a good variety of small stones

✳ one medium-sized rock that is fairly flat

✳ about 6 inches of gray, caulking rope. You can also use modeling clay, but make sure it is *not* the kind that will dry out.

1 Use the medium-sized rock as your base. Next, begin experimenting with designs by balancing different rocks on top of each other. For example, maybe two long stones can be "legs," or maybe you'd rather stack several stones together to create a thick body without legs.

2 If your stones don't quite fit together or won't balance, use a small bit of the caulking rope to fill in the gaps or to get pieces to stick to each other.

3 When you're done, place your inuksuk in a garden or on a windowsill. If you'd like, you can always try your hand at building a full-size inuksuk using larger rocks!

People
Who Work in
Antarctica

Unlike the Arctic region, the continent of Antarctica does not have any native people. Its remote location and brutally cold temperatures don't make it the easiest of places to live. If you need proof, just consider that the biggest native land animal is the half-inch long wingless midge, which is an insect! Penguins are considered ocean animals.

But that doesn't mean there are no people living on Antarctica. Plenty of scientists and other workers live there for part of the year. Some of them even stay year round.

Antarctica doesn't belong to any country, and since it has no native people, it doesn't have a government. For many years, various countries argued over who should control the area. With no rules in place, seal hunters and whalers practically wiped out several species. But then in 1959, twelve countries signed the Antarctic Treaty, agreeing to use the land for peaceful and scientific purposes. For example, the countries all agreed not to test bombs there. These countries include Argentina, Australia, Belgium, Chile, France, Spain, New Zealand, Norway, South Africa, Russia (the former Soviet Union), and the United States of America.

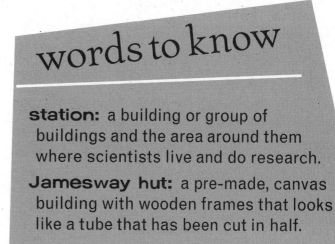

words to know

station: a building or group of buildings and the area around them where scientists live and do research.

Jamesway hut: a pre-made, canvas building with wooden frames that looks like a tube that has been cut in half.

Today, there are sixteen scientific **stations** on Antarctica. Various countries own and operate these stations. Most of the stations are located along the continent's coast or within a hundred miles of it. Two of them, the South Pole Station and the Vostok Station, are located inland, though. Some of the stations are above the ice. Some are buried partially under the ice. Some stations are fairly small, consisting of just a few buildings or Jamesway huts and outhouses. A **Jamesway hut** is a pre-made canvas building with wooden frames. It looks like a tube that has been cut in half. Other stations are large and can accommodate hundreds of people, offering many modern conveniences. Two of the largest stations belong to America. These are the McMurdo Station and the South Pole Station.

The McMurdo Station was established in 1956. It started out as a few buildings on top of exposed rock on the southern tip of Ross Island. Now, it is a small town with nearly one hundred buildings including a church, library, and even a fire station. Like other stations, McMurdo has doctors and cooks and other workers who take care of and support the scientists working there. Instead of traditional houses, everyone lives in dormitories. A dormitory is a residence hall that has lots of bedrooms and shared bathrooms. In the summer months (when tents and Jamesway huts can be used) McMurdo can comfortably house over 1,000 people. During the winter, only about 200 people stay, or **"winter over,"** at the station.

did you know?
At McMurdo Station, boats dock at a pier that is a man-made block of ice.

The Amundsen-Scott South Pole Station, also known simply as the South Pole Station, was first established in 1957. It is not built on land; instead it is built on top of the thick ice. When snow and ice damaged the first buildings, a new station was built in the 1970s. This second station was basically a giant dome that covered several buildings. The dome was 165 feet in diameter and 55 feet tall at its highest point. It wasn't heated, but it did provide a break from the wind and gave the 200 or so scientists and support staff a place to work when there was bad weather. Only about 60 folks stay for the winter.

Eventually, America's National Science Federation decided they needed a bigger and more modern facility. The third South Pole Station opened in 2008 within sight of the old dome. This new station is made of two, blocked "C" shaped units. More units and stories will

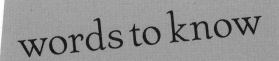

be added as needed. Blowing and piling snow was a problem for the old stations. In fact, the first station is completely buried now. The new station is built on stilts. This way the snow will blow under the building. These hydraulic stilts can also be raised so the building can be used even longer; if the estimates are right, until the year 2050. Despite workers removing it, the snow and ice will pile up about 12 inches a year.

The new station will comfortably house the over 150 **"Polies"** (what the people at the South Pole call themselves) and has many modern comforts including a sauna, galley, and gym. A greenhouse will provide fresh fruit and vegetables. Both the McMurdo and South Pole stations have power plants for electricity. These plants use stored fuel to run generators. The special fuel, which has anti-freeze mixed in to keep it from freezing in the extreme temperatures, is stored in fuel bladders. Bladders look kind of like giant balloons or waterbed mattress. Stations also use solar power.

Life at the Stations

Being in the Antarctic is dangerous. If you're caught outside in a storm you can quickly die. This is why every person who visits or comes to work on the continent must attend **Happy Camper School.** Happy Camper School may sound fun, but it's a survival school. In this "camp," people learn how to survive in the extreme cold and how to avoid dangers like crevasses. For example, campers learn that carrying a water bottle at all times is necessary. This is because dehydration is a real threat; you use a lot of energy moving around and keeping warm. People carry their water bottles inside their coats to keep the water from freezing. Campers also learn how to build an emergency snow dwelling. In order to make sure their snow dwelling is good enough, campers have to spend the night in them!

> ## words to know
>
> **Happy Camper School:** a survival camp where Antarctic visitors learn to survive in the cold and build emergency snow dwellings.
>
> **ozone hole:** a large thinning area in the ozone layer that occurs over the South Pole and parts of the North Pole.
>
> **astrophysicist:** a person who studies what makes up the stars and universe.

The people who work at the McMurdo and South Pole Stations, as well as the other stations on Antarctica, can't run to the store or place an online order when they need something. Because Antarctica is so isolated, stations receive all their supplies from airplanes and boats. The airplanes are mainly LC-130's equipped with skis. Bigger, heavier planes could not land on the ice. Deliveries are made during the summer months. During the dark winter, the weather is too cold and dangerous. So what if someone really needs something, like medicine? One winter, Dr. Jerri Nelson found out she had breast cancer while staying at the South Pole. Airplanes were able to drop boxes with medicine to her, but they couldn't land the plane to pick her up until many months later. Another time, Dr. Ron Shemenski got very ill and needed rescuing, too. Fortunately, the weather cooperated and planes were able to land.

The extreme cold and dry air prevent waste from decomposing in Antarctica. People used to just leave their trash in icy landfills. Today, everyone is making an effort to keep Antarctica and the ocean that surrounds it as clean as possible. The landfills have been cleaned up and all trash, including human waste, is carried off the continent or carefully burned.

Party at the Pole!

Life at the bottom of the world is difficult, but that doesn't mean it's not fun. People who work on Antarctica have many ways to entertain themselves. On their days off, folks go skiing or sledding or stay inside playing board games. Some like to take photographs or play music. Other times, they may have a "beach party" or hold chili cook-offs.

Holidays are celebrated in special ways. For instance, on Christmas, Polies at the South Pole Station hold a "Race Around the World." The outdoor race path goes around the geographic South Pole and the ceremonial South Pole marker. It's called the "Race Around the World" because you're technically going through all time zones. Racers go three laps, or about 2 ½ miles. Because the high altitude makes running difficult, racers don't always actually run. Sometimes they let bulldozers or snowmobiles do the work! And on New Year's Day, the people at the McMurdo Station have a dance and music festival. This event is known as Icestock, a twist on the 1960s music festival Woodstock.

What Are the Scientists Studying?

So just what are the scientists studying at the bottom of the world? A lot of things! Ocean animals such as penguins, plant life, the Earth's magnetosphere, and glaciers. Melting ice and other climate changes, global weather patterns, and Lake Vostok, the 500,000 year-old lake buried under the ice. Because the landscape is barren, similar to the surfaces of other planets, scientists also use the Antarctic to study space exploration. For instance, scientists can test out robotic land explorers to see how well they'll perform in hostile environments.

The skies near the South Pole are very good for studying stars and planets, so many astronomers and **astrophysicists** work there. The South Pole is especially good for viewing stars because there is less water vapor in the air so the air is clearer.

Would You Like to Visit Antarctica?

Scientists and other workers are not the only people who visit Antarctica. These days, it's possible to be a tourist in the coldest place on Earth. There are no hotels on Antarctica, and while it's possible (for a lot of money) to stay at the South Pole Station, most people choose to visit Antarctica by cruise ship. Tourists typically visit the Antarctic Peninsula; other areas are just too hard to get to. These cruise ships usually travel along the coasts or visit the Southern Ocean islands, but occasionally, tourists might visit land for a day. Because Antarctica is so far away, trips to see "The Ice" can cost $10,000 to $20,000 per person. And the trip can be dangerous. In November 2007, the cruise ship *Explorer* sank after hitting ice. Fortunately, none of the passengers or crew was hurt, but they all had to wait for hours in lifeboats in the bitter cold before being rescued.

Secondly, there's no artificial light to distort viewing. And third, in the winter, the stars are visible 24 hours a day! The scientists put up their telescopes and other equipment in a place called "The Dark Sector." This is an area about half mile from South Pole station that is kept free of excess light and electronic transmissions. Less light and electromagnetic pollution helps scientists get more accurate readings.

did you know?
A dozen families live on an Argentinean station on Antarctica. The children attend a small school.

Another very important thing scientists in the Antarctic are studying is Earth's ozone layer. The ozone layer is a special layer of gas in the upper atmosphere that helps block out the harmful ultraviolet rays of the sun. In the 1960s, scientists noticed an alarming thing: every spring, a very large part of the ozone layer thinned out over the Antarctic. This thin area is called the ozone hole. Scientists also discovered that chemicals known as chlorofluorocarbons, or CFCs, were causing the hole. Since the 1970s, CFCs, which used to be in things like aerosol spray cans and car exhaust, have been phased out completely. Scientists are hopeful that the ozone hole will eventually fix itself. There is also an ozone hole above the Arctic but it's much smaller and not as big a concern.

More
Things to Try

- Everyone who lives at a station takes turns being the "house mouse," helping out with the cooking and cleaning. Create a family or classroom chore chart and take turns being the house mouse.

- On January 7, 1978, Emilio de Palma was the first person to do something on Antarctica. See if you can find out what his claim to fame is.

Make Your Own
Ceremonial South Pole Marker

Many people who go to the South Pole have their picture taken in front of the barbershop-style pole that ceremoniously marks the spot. The real, geographic South Pole moves slightly each year and is marked by a plaque. Here's a fun way to make your own ceremonial South Pole marker. You can take it outside in the snow if you'd like to create a "South Pole" photo, but you shouldn't leave it outside permanently. You'll be using a hot glue gun and spray paint for this project so ask an adult to help.

1 Wrap the red duct tape around the PVC pipe in a barbershop-pole fashion. If you don't have tape, use a red marker to create the twisting lines.

2 Paint both sides of the cardboard circle with the gray paint and allow it to dry. Once it's dry, hot glue the PVC pipe to the center of the cardboard circle. Turn the pole so that the cardboard sits on top of the pole. Set aside for the time being.

Supplies

❄ red duct tape or a permanent red marker

❄ PVC pipe, 4 inches in diameter and $2^1/_2$ feet long, found at many hardware stores*

❄ cardboard circle, 12 inches in diameter

❄ gray paint

❄ hot glue gun

❄ lots of newspaper

❄ inexpensive plastic ball, about 10 inches in diameter

❄ small plastic container

❄ 2 cups water

❄ 1 cup flour

❄ small bowl

❄ metallic silver spray paint

3 Cover your work area with newspaper. Set the ball on top of the newspapers. Set it on top of a small plastic container to keep it from rolling.

4 Tear several sections of newspaper into strips that are several inches long. Mix the flour and water together in the bowl to create your own papier-mâché.

5 Dip a few strips of the newspaper into the papier-mâché. Remove any extra liquid by gently running the newspaper strips through your fingers. Begin covering the ball with the strips.

6 Continue covering the ball with pieces of newspaper until it's completely covered. Don't forget to turn the ball over so you get the bottom covered, too. Put several layers of newspaper on the ball. Allow the ball to dry for several days.

7 When the ball is ready, follow the directions on the spray can and paint the ball metallic silver. Allow it to dry. Then use a small bit of hot glue to secure the silver ball to the top of the cardboard circle.

8 Now your South Pole marker is ready! If you want to take it outside and it won't stand up in the snow or on uneven ground, simply place the bottom of the pole into a large coffee can that's been filled with beans.

* Variation: Some stores don't sell PVC by the foot. If you can't find PVC pipe, you can use an empty cardboard roll from carpet or upholstery. You can sometimes get these for free by just asking for them at the store. You can also roll up a piece of poster board lengthwise and tape it closed, or use a large poster mailer, which you can find at an office supply store or the post office. Just paint these rolls white before adding the red stripe.

Make Your Own
Neck Gator

Everyone who works on Antarctica gets special warm clothing called Extreme Cold Weather gear, or ECW gear. One of the items is a pair of insulated, white rubber boots called Bunny Boots. Another item is a neck gator. A neck gator is a warm tube that goes around your neck to help block out the wind and the cold. You'll be using a sewing machine for this project, so ask an adult for help.

Supplies
* stretchy fleece, 21 inches long by 12 inches tall
* scissors
* sewing machine

1 Lay your material with the long ends at the top and bottom. Next, fold the top edge down and sew a 1-inch seam along the top of the material. Fold the bottom edge up and sew a 1-inch seam along the bottom of the material. Next, turn the material over so the seams are facing down.

2 Fold the material over to the right so that you have a rectangle approximately 10½ inches wide and 10 inches tall. Now you can see part of the seams again at the top and bottom.

3 Sew a straight line along the right edge, the one that is opposite the fold. The seam should be about 1-inch from the edge. When you're done, you should have a material tube. Turn the material tube inside out so that all the seams are in the inside.

4 Now, you're ready to go! To put your neck gator on, simply pull it over your head and let it wrap around your neck. For extra warmth you can pull part of the neck gator up over your mouth and nose.

* Important note: The stretch of the fabric must be going the long way of the rectangle. The stretch of fleece should go from the uncut edges of the fabric. To make sure you've got it, gently pull the fabric from side to side and then from top to bottom. One direction should "give" a little more than the other. The side that gives more is the "stretch." If you don't have the stretch going the right way, it will be too hard to pull your neck gator over your head.

Make Your Own
Jar Terrarium

The South Pole Station has an indoor greenhouse to grow fresh fruits, vegetables, and herbs for the people who work there. Without it, everyone at the station would have to eat canned and dried foods for months. Boring! Here is a simple way to make your own self-contained garden, or terrarium, so you can enjoy herbs even if it's cold outside.

1 Before you begin, you need to sterilize the jar and lid. The easiest way to do this is to run them both through the dishwasher. You can also just wash them thoroughly using hot water and soap.

2 Once your jar is clean, pour in the aquarium gravel. The gravel will help with drainage. Add the charcoal to keep the air fresh.

3 Add the moss or screen. This layer helps keep the soil from settling down into the rocks and charcoal. Finally, add the soil. You'll need about 2 to 3 inches of it.

4 Now you can plant your herb plant. When you're done, water the plant according to the directions on the plant card or seed packet.

Supplies

* large *clear* glass jar, with lid
* ¼ cup aquarium gravel
* ⅛ cup aquarium charcoal
* sphagnum moss or a piece of screen cut to the diameter of the jar
* ½ cup to 1 cup potting soil
* small herb plant such as basil, cilantro, sage, thyme, or dill

5 Put your jar on a windowsill that gets lots of sun. Whether or not you put the lid on the terrarium and how much you water it depends on what kind of herb you plant. Most herbs like humidity, so lightly screw the lid on the jar. You'll need to take the lid off every once in a while so the air inside the jar doesn't get too moist or too hot. If your herb doesn't like humidity, simply leave the lid off. Mist or sprinkle the plant with water as needed.

Taking Care of the Poles

Many experts describe the Arctic and Antarctic as Earth's air conditioners. This is because the polar regions help regulate the planet's temperature. What happens to them affects everyone. And this is why we need to take care of them and pay attention to when, and how, they change. Lately, there is a lot of information about global warming and climate change. What do these things mean? How are they affecting the Poles? And, more importantly, are there things we can do to help protect the Arctic and Antarctic?

Global Warming and Climate Change

Global warming and **climate change** are two different, but related, things. Global warming is the rise of the earth's average air temperature. More accurately, it's the rise of temperature near the planet's surface and in the **troposphere**, or the lower atmosphere. **Climate** is the long-term weather pattern for a particular geographic area. And climate change is a big change to a climate that lasts over a long period of time. Earth's climates work in cycles. For example, hot to cold and then cold to hot, rainy to dry and dry to wet. Global warming can cause climate change.

You might have heard about the **Greenhouse Effect**. This is not a bad thing; it's how the earth keeps itself at a temperature comfortable for human, animal, and plant life. This is how it works: the earth has an atmosphere, or layer of gases, high above it. It's kind of like a protective bubble around the earth. The sun's energy passes through the atmosphere and warms the surface of the planet. Some of the sun's energy is reflected off the earth and radiated back into space. But some of it is trapped by the atmosphere.

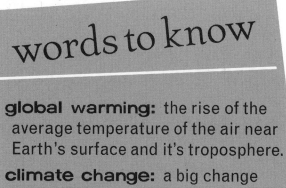

words to know

global warming: the rise of the average temperature of the air near Earth's surface and it's troposphere.

climate change: a big change to the climate that lasts over a long period of time.

troposphere: Earth's lower atmosphere.

climate: the long-term weather patterns of a particular area of land.

Greenhouse Effect: a natural occurrence where the atmosphere traps the sun's energy and keeps the planet comfortable for human, animal, and plant life.

And, just as the inside of a car or a greenhouse heats up when they are closed, the earth gets warmer. This is how the Greenhouse Effect gets its name. Our planet would be about 60 degrees colder without the

Greenhouse Effect. The problem is that the atmosphere is getting thicker and more energy is getting trapped inside, unable to pass through the atmosphere and back out into space. This means the earth is getting warmer. And warmer temperatures may be causing more extreme weather such as stronger and more frequent hurricanes and heat waves.

Why is the atmosphere getting thicker? Well, that's been the big question for the last couple of decades. **Climatologists** agree that humans are releasing too many manmade greenhouse gases into the atmosphere and causing the change to the delicate system. The main greenhouse gases include water vapor, methane, and nitrous oxide. The most common greenhouse gas, though, is carbon dioxide or CO_2. Some carbon dioxide occurs naturally. For example, when humans and animal exhale. But humans create most of it when we burn fossil fuels, burn forests, or drive cars. And in the last 200 years or so since the **Industrial Revolution** (in other words, since we've started building factories and using powered machines) we have been producing more CO_2 than any other time in history.

did you know?
Some experts predict that within the century, the Arctic Ocean won't have any ice during the summer months.

words to know

climatologists: people who study climates.

Industrial Revolution: the time in history when power-driven machinery changed the way countries produced goods. This happened in the late 1700s in the United States.

How Are the Arctic and Antarctic Affected?

The polar regions are feeling the effects of global warming and climate change, especially the Arctic. This is because the Arctic's ice is thinner than in Antarctica.

The biggest concern for the Arctic is that the ice cap is melting—and quickly. According to NASA's studies, it's decreasing by about 9 percent each decade and is currently at record lows. Global warming has caused the ice to melt, but feedback is also a problem. Feedback basically means that as more ice melts, the rate of melting increases.

did you know?
If all the land ice on Earth melted, the ocean level would rise to dangerous levels and cause flooding all over the world. Fortunately, this isn't likely to happen for a long time. Scientists are researching just how fast the ice is melting and what we can do about it.

Ice reflects the sun's energy and helps keep the air colder but less ice means more of the sun's energy is hitting, and heating, the ocean where the ice is floating. Warmer ocean water means more ice melts. More melting ice means more of the ocean is exposed, and so on.

Even if all the ice in the Arctic melted, it wouldn't cause the ocean level to rise and lands to flood. This is because the ice was created from water that was already in the ocean. But though melting ice doesn't affect ocean levels, thinning ice definitely affects the animals that depend on it. For example, polar bears use the ice floes to travel and rest while they're looking for seals and other prey. This means polar bears must swim for longer distances and some of them might

Questions about Global Warming

While scientists agree that the Earth is getting warmer, a few disagree about what this will mean for life in the future. They wonder if the climate changes the Earth is experiencing are caused by humans or are a part of a natural cycle. They also are unsure about what we should do, if anything, about global warming. Sorting everything out can be confusing. This is why scientists, climatologists, and world leaders everywhere are working towards finding more answers. In the meantime, we can all agree on this: taking care of our planet by recycling and reducing pollution is always a good idea!

drown, unable to make it all the way. The thinning ice also changes the migration patterns of ocean animals such as whales and seals. This makes it hard for the Inuit (and polar bears) to hunt them. The mating seasons of animals are also affected, and babies are being born when there is less food.

The Arctic tundra is also feeling the effects of global warming. The frozen layer of soil, or permafrost, is melting. This is causing plant life or manmade structures like buildings and

 the Alaskan Pipeline to lean or fall over. It is causing sinkholes and flooding. Melting ice in the permafrost is also causing the release of methane. All this methane (from the decay of plants and animals that were frozen in the ice) is adding to the greenhouse gases and, in turn, raising temperatures further.

Antarctica seems to be less affected by global warming than its northern counterpart. This is because Antarctica is colder than the Arctic and the ice on Antarctica is on top of land. Plus, there is a lot of ice! These factors mean it would take a long time for the ice on Antarctica to melt. But scientists are still concerned. For instance, there have been some unusually large icebergs breaking off into the ocean. The ice shelf in the Antarctic peninsula has broken up, too. Scientists are wondering if natural cycles caused these things or if global warming did—or at least played a role.

Another concern is the decrease in krill in the peninsula area. Less krill and less ice have made it harder for Adelie penguins to survive. Scientists aren't entirely sure what is causing this either.

What Can We Do?

People all over the world are studying global warming and climate change and figuring out what we can do about them. Many countries have promised to work together. The Kyoto Protocol, for instance, is an agreement that dozens of countries signed in Kyoto, Japan in 1997. This agreement outlines ways countries can reduce their CO_2 emissions. Though the United States is not part of this agreement for a variety of reasons, numerous states have acted on their own to lower CO_2 emissions. There is also a group known as the Intergovernmental Panel on Climate Change, or IPCC for short, which is committed to colleting and studying information from scientists all around the world and presenting the findings objectively.

Getting Everyone Together

In the last 100 years, countries have come together to focus on the polar regions four times. The first International Polar Year (1882-83) was inspired by an Australian explorer named Lt. Karl Weyprecht. The goal of this program, along with later ones in the years 1932-33 and 1957-58, was to coordinate scientific research in the Arctic and Antarctic and share information among numerous countries. Organized by the International Council for Science and the World Meteorological Organization, the most recent International Polar Year (which studied two seasonal cycles) was in 2007-2009 and included thousands of scientists from over 60 nations.

Even if you're not a scientist or world leader, there are still plenty of things you can do to help the environment and protect the polar regions. Here are just a few ideas:

Recycle. Don't throw out glass, newspapers, cardboard, plastic, and other things that can be recycled. Don't have a recycling program at home or at school? Start one!

Reduce your waste and reuse materials. Don't be wasteful. For example, use both sides of paper or use the same lunch bag all week. Don't throw out old cell phones or toys; donate them to someone who needs them.

Encourage your parents to use compact fluorescent bulbs. These bulbs last longer and help the environment.

Walk or bike more often. Less driving means less CO_2 in the air.

Save electricity. Turn things off when you're not using them. Unplug unused appliances so they don't drain electricity.

Take showers, not baths. Showers use less water.

Plant trees. They help reduce CO_2 in the air.

Be a good consumer. Buy toys, CDs, and other things that don't have a lot of packaging. Or make gifts for birthdays and holidays.

Spread the word about protecting the Poles and the wildlife that live in these areas.

More Things to Try

- Play "The New Use" game to see how many different ways can you use something. Pick an item such as a milk jug or egg carton and have a contest with your family and friends, making a list of new uses for the item. If an idea is repeated, everyone must cross it off their lists. The person with the most original new uses wins that round.

- Learn more about the International Polar Year by visiting www.IPY.org.

Experiment with **Warmer Temperatures and Ice**

In the last hundred years or so, Earth's average temperatures have risen about a couple degrees. Scientists predict that if global warming continues, the temperature could rise 3 to 7 degrees Fahrenheit by the end of the century. Can a few degrees really make a difference at the Poles? Here's a simple experiment that tests this question.

1 Fill each container with 1 cup of water. Put one container in the refrigerator. Put the other container of water in a sunny spot indoors. Don't put the container outside or too close to a window or the air temperature may affect it. Set the timer for 5 minutes.

2 After the timer goes off, remove the container from the refrigerator. Place it next to the container in the sunny spot. If you'd like to measure the temperature of the water in each container, now is the time to do so. Refrigerators' temperatures vary, but the difference between the water that's been in the sun and the water that's been in the refrigerator should be about 3 to 5 degrees. You can also put both containers in a spot that's not sunny for the next step. They just have to be exposed to the same amount of light.

3 Place an ice cube in each container and observe. Which ice cube melts faster? Does it melt a little bit faster or a lot faster?

Supplies

❋ two identical plastic containers

❋ water

❋ measuring cup

❋ timer

❋ refrigerator

❋ a sunny day

❋ scientific or aquarium thermometer (optional)

❋ two identical ice cubes

What's happening?

The water that's been in the sun, even though it's just a few degrees warmer, melts the ice much quicker than the water that's cooler. Think about what this means for the ice at the Poles. It takes only a few minutes to melt one ice cube. Imagine how much polar ice is melting in just one year's time!

Make Your Own
Earth Pin

Show your support for the earth (and do some recycling) by creating your own shirt or jacket pin. Perhaps you can even make several pins and sell them to family and friends to raise money for an environmental organization or a group that is helping polar animals.

Supplies

* orange juice can lid, clean and dried, or a 2-inch circle out of cardboard or a plastic container lid

* 1 piece of thick, white drawing paper

* markers

* scissors

* craft glue

* clear Contact paper

* pre-made pin with adhesive back found at a craft store in the jewelry aisle

1 Lay your lid on top of the paper and trace a circle. Cut out the paper circle so that it is about ¼ inch smaller that your lid.

2 Next, create an earth-friendly design or motto on the paper circle. Get creative! Maybe you can simply draw the earth or a smiling earth to remind people to take care of our planet. Or draw a picture of someone recycling or riding a bike. Maybe you can come up with some catchy phrase. For instance, "Polar Ice is Nice!" When you're happy with your design, glue it on top of the lid.

3 Next, lay the lid on top of the Contact paper. Trace a circle and cut it out. Pull the protective layer off the back of the Contact™ paper and lay it sticky-side down on top of your picture. This will help protect your design.

4 Finally, peel the backing off the pin and secure it to the back of your lid. Now you're ready to show the world you care!

Glossary

active layer: the top layer of soil in the Arctic Circle that defrosts each summer.

adaptations: changes an animal or plant makes (or has) in response to its environment.

Adelie: one of the two species of penguins that live on Antarctica.

air hole: a hole made in the ice by animals that must come up to breath.

Antarctic: the region at the bottom of the Southern Hemisphere.

Antarctic Circle: an imaginary circle that extends north about 1,620 miles in every direction from the geographic South Pole.

Antarctica: one of the seven continents of the world and the most southern.

Arctic: the region at the top of the Northern Hemisphere.

Arctic Circle: an imaginary circle that extends south about 1,620 miles in every direction from the geographic North Pole.

Arctic tundra: the treeless area that encircles the North Pole and extends down to the forest areas of North America, Europe, and other areas in the Arctic Circle.

astrophysicist: a person who studies what makes up the stars and universe.

atmosphere: the air or gas surrounding a planet.

atom: a small particle of matter.

aurora: a colorful light show caused by particles from solar winds colliding with the earth's atmosphere.

axis: the imaginary line that the earth rotates around.

baleen plates: sections of long, fringe-like material that hangs from a whale's jaw and helps it eat.

biome: a particular climate and its plants and animals. Deserts and rainforests are examples of biomes.

blubber: a layer of fat under a marine mammal's skin used to help keep the animal warm.

calving: the breaking apart of a glacier.

camouflage: protective coloration that helps a plant or animal hide and survive in its environment.

Chukchi: the native people of the northeasternmost part of Siberia.

climate: the long-term weather patterns of a particular area of land.

climate change: a big change to the climate that lasts over a long period of time.

climatologists: people who study climates.

colony: a community of penguins.

crevasses: deep cracks in the tops of glaciers.

cub: baby bear.

down: soft, fine feathers.

Dry Valleys: extremely cold mountain valleys with dry, bare rock and soil. The Dry Valleys are located just west of McMurdo Sound on East Antarctica.

ecosystem: a community of plants and animals living in the same area and relying on each other to survive.

Emperor: one of the two species of penguins that live on Antarctica.

endangered: species of animals or plants that are in danger of going extinct.

equator: the imaginary line running around the middle of the earth that divides it into the Northern Hemisphere and the Southern Hemisphere.

equinox: the two days of the year when days and nights are equal lengths.

fast ice: sea ice that extends from the coasts of Antarctica like a shelf.

firn: grain-like snow crystals.

Glossary

floe: large, flat pieces of sea ice.

glacier: a very large field of fresh water ice that is moving.

global warming: an increase in the average temperature of the earth's atmosphere, causing climatic change.

grease ice: a slushy, soupy ice that leaves an oily sheen on top of the water. It is the first stage of sea ice.

Greenhouse Effect: a natural occurrence where the atmosphere traps the sun's energy and keeps the planet comfortable for human, animal, and plant life.

halos: displays of light that are created when light is bent while going through ice crystals or cirrus clouds. They often look like rings or light or color around the sun or moon.

Happy Camper School: a survival camp where Antarctic visitors learn to survive in the cold and build emergency snow dwellings.

haul out: to climb out of the water.

hemisphere: half a sphere, like half a ball.

hypothermia: when the body's temperature falls below 95 degrees.

ice wedge: a wedge-shaped piece of ice that forms in the active layer of the tundra. When they push the surrounding soil up and out, they form tundra polygons.

iceberg: a piece of ice that's broken off a glacier and is floating in the ocean.

igloo: a temporary, Inuit dwelling made out of blocks of snow.

indicator species: an animal so in tune with its environment that even a tiny change in the environment can put the species in danger.

Industrial Revolution: the time in history when power-driven machinery changed the way countries produced goods. This happened in the late 1700s in the United States.

Inuit: the native people who live in the Arctic tundra, Northern Canada, Russia, Greenland, and Alaska.

Jamesway hut: a pre-made, canvas building with wooden frames that looks like a tube that has been cut in half.

katabtic winds: high-speed winds that constantly race down mountain slopes.

kayak: a single person boat that is completely enclosed except for the space wear the rower sits.

keels: the ice that is pushed underwater when ice floes collide.

krill: a small, shrimp-like creature.

latitude: how far north or south a location is from the equator.

Little Ice Age: a period of time that began about 700 years ago when the temperatures in the Northern Hemisphere began to cool down.

logbook: a notebook or journal that sailors, pilots, and other explorers use to record daily details about their travels.

magnetic field: an invisible field (or area) created by moving charges near a magnet or an electrical current.

Magnetic North Pole: the northernmost point of the earth's magnetic field.

Magnetic South Pole: the southernmost point of the earth's magnetic field.

marine mammal: an animal that gives birth, nurses its young, and can maintain a constant body temperature. It also lives in or near the sea and relies on the sea for food.

migrate: to move or travel from place to another.

molting: process in which a bird's old feathers are pushed out by new feathers growing in.

Glossary

Nanook: what the Inuit people call the polar bear. It means "He who is without shadow."

nilas: the second stage of sea ice formation, this thin, flexible sheet of ice moves with the waves.

North Pole: the northernmost point on the earth, also called the geographic North Pole.

Northern Hemisphere: the top half of the globe.

Northern Lights: the auroras that occur in the Northern Hemisphere.

ozone hole: a large thinning area in the ozone layer that occurs over the South Pole and parts of the North Pole.

ozone: a kind of oxygen with three molecules that forms the ozone layer.

pancake ice: the third stage of sea ice. These large plates of ice bump into each other and cause the edges to turn up.

pennipeds: aquatic animals that use flippers to swim or move on land. The word means "wing-footed."

permafrost: a layer of soil in the Arctic Circle that's permanently frozen.

poaching: breaking the rules and hunting where and when you're not supposed to.

pod: a group of whales.

polar ice cap: a giant sheet of sea ice that floats on top of the Arctic Ocean.

Polies: what the people who work at the South Pole station call themselves.

precipitation: rain or snow.

rookeries: areas where penguins set up nests.

Sami: the native people who live in Sweden, Norway, Finland, and the Kola Peninsula of Russia.

scurvy: a serious illness caused by a lack of vitamin C in someone's diet. It's common in sailors and others who go a long time without fresh fruit.

sea ice: ice made up of ocean water.

shaman: a wise leader, who native people believe has special powers and can connect to the spiritual world.

solar wind: the stream of electrically charged particles emitted by the sun.

solstice: the two times of the year when the sun is at its highest and lowest points in the sky.

South Pole: the southernmost point on the earth, also called the geographic South Pole.

Southern Hemisphere: the bottom half of the globe.

Southern Lights: the auroras that occur in the Southern Hemisphere.

station: a building or group of buildings and the area around them where scientists live and do research.

The Ice: nickname for Antarctica.

threatened species: an animal whose existence is threatened.

toboggan: a kind of sled.

troposphere: Earth's lower atmosphere.

tundra polygon: block-shaped patterns that form on the tundra's surface when ice wedges displace soil.

tundra: the treeless plain area between the ice of the Arctic and the forests of northern lands.

umiaks: big, rowboat-like boats that the Inuit used to hunt whales and to move their families.

vegetation: all the plant life in a particular area.

ventifacts: rocks that have been smoothed and shaped over time by wind and ice crystals.

walking hibernation: a state where a polar bear's metabolism, heart, and breathing rate slow down as a way to conserve energy during times where food is harder to find.

winter over: to stay in the Antarctic during the winter months.

Resources

For additional resources, please visit http://www.nomadpress.net/childrens/buildIt/books/amazing_arctic_antarctic.html

Books

Armstrong, Jennifer. *Shipwreck at the Bottom of the World.* Crown Publishers, 1998.

Billings, Henry. *Enchantment of the World: Antarctica.* Children's Press, 1994.

Bledsoe, Lucy Jane. *How to Survive in Antarctica.* Holiday House, 2006.

Dingwall, Laima. *Nature's Children: Walrus.* Grolier Educational, 1986.

Feazel, Charles. T., *White Bear.* Henry Holt Company, 1990.

Gore, Al. *An Inconvenient Truth.* Rodale, 2006.

Grupper, Jonathan. *Destination Polar Regions.* National Geographic, 1999.

Lewis, Jon. E. (editor) *The Mammoth Book of Polar Journeys.* Carroll and Graf, 2007.

Loewn, Nancy and Bancroft, Ann. *Four to the Pole: The American Women's Expedition to Antarctica, 1992-93.* Linnet Books, 2001.

Love, Ann and Drake, Jane. *The Kids Book of The Far North.* Kids Can Press, 2000.

Lynch, Wayne. *Arctic Alphabet.* Firefly Books, 1999.

Lynch, Wayne. *Penguins of the World.* Firefly Books, 1997.

Matthews, Down. *Polar Bears.* Chronicle Books, 1993.

Miller, Debbie S. *Arctic Lights Arctic Nights.* Walker and Company, 2003.

Pringle, Laurence. *Penguins! Strange and Wonderful.* Boyds Mills Press, 2007.

Revkin, Andrew C., *The North Pole Was Here.* Kingfisher, 2006.

Scott, Elaine. *Poles Apart.* Viking, 2004.

Simon, Seymour. *Icebergs and Glaciers.* Mulberry Books, 1987.

Stefoff, Rebecca. *Animal Ways: Penguins.* Marshall Cavendish, 2005.

Taylor, Barbara. *DK Eyewitness Books: Arctic and Antarctic.* Dorling Kindersley, 1995.

Williams, Jack. *The Complete Idiot's Guide to the Arctic and Antarctic.* Alpha, 2003.

Articles

Associated Press. "Canada restakes claim to Arctic." *The Columbus Dispatch*, August 9, 2007.

Begley, Sharon. "The Truth About Denial." *Newsweek*, August 13, 2007.

Bowley, Graham & Revkin, Andrew. "Antarctic cruise ship hits ice, sinks." *New York Times*, November 24, 2007.

Casey, Michael. "Species taking a beating as temperatures creep higher." *The Columbus Dispatch*, December 6, 2007.

Diegel, Angela & Rubin, Jeff. "South Pole Amundsen-Scott Research Station." *Popular Mechanics*, Sept., 2005.

Engeler, Elaine. "Carbon dioxide hit[s] high in '06 U.N. says." *The Columbus Dispatch*, November 24, 2007.

Esser, Doug (Associate Press). "U.S. icebreaker to map Arctic sea flour." *Yahoo! News*, August, 10, 2007.

Ferdinand, Pamela. "A flexible, 9 foot whale tooth with super-sensing power?" *National Geographic News* (www.news.nationalgeographic.com) Dec. 13, 2005.

Helmuth, Laura. "Antarctica Erupts!" Smithsonian, Dec. 2006.

Max, Arthur. "Dire events follow inaction, climate-change panel says." *The Columbus Dispatch*, November 18, 2007.

Mullen, William. "An Ominous Thaw." *The Columbus Dispatch*, July 15, 2007.

Roach, John. "Penguin Decline Due to Global Warming?" *National Geographic News*, Sept. 13, 2004.

Roach, John. "Global Warming is Rapidly Raising Sea Levels." *National Geographic News*, March 23, 2006.

Vedantam, Shankar. "Kyoto Treaty Takes Effect Today." *Washington Post*, February 16, 2005.

Documentaries

"A Global Warning?" (2007) History Channel. Produced by Pioneer Productions.

"Blue Planet: Frozen Seas" (2007) Discovery Channel. Produced by Dr. Martha Holmes.

"Emperors of the Ice" (2006) National Geographic Television and Film. Produced by Greg Marshall.

"March of the Penguins" (2005) Warner Films. Directed by Luc Jacquet.

"Masters of the Arctic Ice" (2007) National Geographic Television and Film. Produced be Greg Marshall.

Websites
General information

www.educapoles.org

www.athropolis.com/

www.coolantarctica.com

www.seaworld.org

www.soundswild.alaska.gov

www.adfg.state.ak.us

www.ipy.org

Index

Index